Smart Travel 13 National Parks in the Mountain West

Camping & Hiking Guide

(Also In –Depth Guide to Arches, Bryce Canyon, Grand Teton, Yellowstone, Zion, Rocky Mountain & Glacier National Parks)

BY

Rob J. Simms

Copyrighted Material

*Copyright © 2018 – **CSBA Publishing House***

Email:csbapublishing@gmail.com

All Rights Reserved.

No part of this publication may be reproduced, stored in a retrieval system or transmitted in any form or by any means, electronic, mechanical, photocopying, recording or otherwise without the proper written consent of the copyright holder, except brief quotations used in a review.

Published by:

CSBA Publishing House

Cover & Interior designed

By

Denise Nicholson

First Edition

CONTENTS

Acknowledgements 11
Introduction 12
Part – 1 13
13 National Parks in the Mountain West 13
Carlsbad Caverns, New Mexico 14
Arches, Utah 19
Bryce Canyon, Utah 23
Canyonlands, Utah 27
Capitol Reef, Utah 31
Zion National Park, Utah 34
Rocky Mountain, Colorado 38
Mesa Verde, Colorado 43
Great Sand Dunes, Colorado 48
Black Canyon of the Gunnison, Colorado 52
Yellowstone Idaho/Montana/Wyoming 56
Grand Teton, Wyoming 61
Glacier, Montana 65
Part -2 69
What to See and Do in a Day Trip 69
Carlsbad Caverns, New Mexico 70
Arches, Utah 73
    Viewing the Park by Car 73
    Day Hikes in the Park 74

Bryce Canyon, Utah 76
Canyonlands, Utah 78
    Islands in the Sky District 79
    The Needles District 79

Capitol Reef, Utah 80
    Scenic Drive 80
    South Draw Road 80
    Notom-Bullfrog Road 81
    Burr Trail Road 81
    Hartnet Road 81
    Cathedral Road 82

Zion, Utah 83
Rocky Mountain, Colorado 85

- Mesa Verde, Colorado 88
- Great Sand Dunes, Colorado 91
- Black Canyon of the Gunnison, Colorado 93
  - South Rim Road 93
  - North Rim Road 94
  - East Portal Road 94
- Yellowstone, Idaho/Montana/Wyoming 95
- Grand Teton, Wyoming 98
  - Scenic Drives 98
  - Wildlife Viewing 99
- Glacier, Montana 102

Part – 3 104
- 14-Day Park Hopper Travel Plans 104
- 2-Week Trip Itineraries 104
- Itinerary #1: Colorado 105
  - Great Sand Dunes, Mesa Verde, Black Canyon of the Gunnison, Rocky Mountain 105
  - Great Sand Dunes 105
    - Forested Trails 106
    - Alpine Trails 107
  - Mesa Verde 108
    - Guided Tours 109
    - Self-Guided Tours 110
    - Hiking Trails 111
  - Black Canyon of the Gunnison 113
    - South Rim 113
    - North Rim 114
    - Inner Canyon Hiking 115
    - Routes Along the North Rim 116
    - Routes Along the South Rim 117
    - Routes Along the East Portal 118
  - Rocky Mountain 118
    - Lake Hike Chart 119
    - Waterfall Hike Chart 120
    - Summit Hike Chart 120
- Itinerary #2: Utah 121

Arches, Canyonlands, Capitol Reef, Bryce Canyon, Zion 121
Arches 121
    Park Avenue and Courthouse Towers 121
    Balanced Rock 122
    The Windows Section 122
    Delicate Arch 123
    Devil's Garden 124

Canyonlands 126
Capitol Reef 128
Three Types of Hiking Trails (Easy, Moderate & Strenuous) 129
    Easy Hikes 129
    Moderate Hikes 130
    Strenuous Hikes 130

Bryce Canyon 131
    Geology Talks 131
    Rim Walk 131
    Kids Programs 132
    Evening Programs 132
    Full Moon Hikes 132
    Astronomy Programs 132
    Snowshoe Hikes 133

Zion 133
    The Narrows 133
    Kolob Canyons 135

Part – 4 136
A Detail In-Depth Look Inside 7 Most Popular Parks 136
In –Depth Guide to Arches, Bryce Canyon, Grand Teton, Yellowstone, Zion, Rocky Mountain & Glacier National Parks 136
In-Depth Guide to Arches National Park 137
  Activities 137
  Backpacking 137
    Permits 138
    Requirements 138
    Safety 139
    Backcountry Camping 140

  Biking 140
  Canyoneering 140

- Regulations 141
- Registration 142
- Safety 143
- Canyoneering Routes 143

Commercial Tours 144
Hiking 144
- Easy Hikes 144
- Moderate Hikes 145
- Strenuous Hikes 145

Horseback Riding 145
Rock Climbing 147
- Regulations 147
- Registration 147
- Safety 148
- Rock Climbing Routes 148

In-Depth Guide to Bryce Canyon National Park 150

Festivals 150
- Geology Festival 150
- Prairie Dog Festival 150
- Astronomy Festival 150

Hiking Trails 151
Easy Hiking Trails 151
- Mossy Cave 151
- Rim Trail 152
- Bristlecone Loop 152
- Queens Garden 152

Moderate Hiking Trails 152
- Navajo Trail 152
- Tower Bridge 153
- Hat Shop 153
- Swamp Canyon 153

Strenuous Hiking Trails 154
- Fairyland Loop 154
- Peek-A-Boo Loop 154
- Riggs Spring Loop 154

In-Depth Guide to Zion National Park 156

- Activities 156
- Backpacking Trail Options 156
  - East Rim Trail 156
  - Hop Valley Trail 157
  - La Verkin Creek Trail 158
  - Southwest Desert (Chinle Trail and Coalpits Wash) 158
  - The Narrows at the North Fork of the Virgin River 159
  - West Rim Trail 159
  - Wildcat Canyon Trail 160
- Hiking 160
  - Easy Trails 160
  - Moderate Trails 161
  - Strenuous Trails 161

In-Depth Guide to Rocky Mountain National Park 162

- A Week in Rocky Mountain 162
  - Day One 162
  - Day Two 162
  - Day Three 162
  - Day Four 163
  - Day Five 163
  - Day Six 163
  - Day Seven 163
- Hiking 164
  - Lake Hiking Chart 164
  - Waterfall Hiking Chart 166
  - Mountain Summits Hiking Chart 167

In-Depth Guide to Yellowstone National Park 168

- Fishing Bridge, Lake Village, and Bridge Bay Area 168
  - View Fish at Fishing Bridge 168
  - Yellowstone Lake 168
  - Visit the Mud Volcano 169
  - Wildlife Viewing in Hayden and Pelican Valleys 169
  - Hike to Natural Bridge 169
- Canyon Village 170
  - Hike to Artist's Point 170
  - Wildlife Viewing in Hayden Valley 170

  Stop by the Canyon Visitor Education Center 170
  Take in the Views from Mt. Washburn 171

West Thumb and Grant Village 171

  View Yellowstone Lake 171
  View West Thumb Geyser Basin 171
  Learn About the Early Inhabitants 172
  Stop by the Grant Village Visitor Center 172
  Stop by the West Thumb Information Station 172
  Hike to Shoshone Lake and the Snake River 173

Madison and West Yellowstone 173

  Stop by the Madison Information Station 173
  Hike to Artists Paintpots 173
  Hike to Gibbon Falls 174
  Hike to Monument Geyser Basin 174
  Fish in the Madison River 174
  Tour the Terrace Springs Boardwalk 174
  Fish in the Firehole River 174
  Drive Firehole Canyon and Swim Firehole Falls 174

Mammoth Hot Springs 175

  Stop by the Albright Visitor Center 175
  Take a Historic Tour of Fort Yellowstone 175
  Walk the Mammoth Hot Springs Terraces 175
  Take a Hike 175
  Hike, Bike, or Drive Old Gardiner Road 176
  Visit the Heritage and Research Center 176

Norris 176

  Walk the Norris Geyser Basin Boardwalks 176
  Hike to Roaring Mountain 177
  Fish in the Gibbon River 177
  Drive the Virginia Cascades 177
  View the Norris-Canyon Blowdown 177
  Visit the Norris Geyser Basin Museum 178
  Visit the Museum of the National Park Ranger 178

Old Faithful 178

  View the Old Faithful Inn 179
  Hike the Upper Geyser Basin 179
  Visit Midway Geyser Basin 179

Visit the Lower Geyser Basin 179
　　Hike to Lone Star Geyser 180
　　See an Old Faithful Eruption 180
　Tower-Roosevelt 180
　　Day Hike to Tower Fall 180
　　Stop at Calcite Springs Overlook 181
　　Take a Class at the Lamar Buffalo Ranch 181
　　Visit Roosevelt Lodge 181
　　Enjoy Dinner in Pleasant Valley 182
　　Hike the Bannock Trail 182
In-Depth Guide to Grand Teton National Park 183
　Moose District 183
　Colter Bay 184
　Jenny Lake 186
　Laurance S. Rockefeller District 187
In-Depth Guide to Glacier National Park 189
　Lake McDonald Valley 189
　Facilities, Services, and Activities 190
　　Hikes 190
　Logan Pass 191
　　Facilities, Services, and Activities 192
　　Hikes 192
　Many Glacier 192
　　Facilities, Services, and Activities 193
　　Hikes 194
　St. Mary Valley 195
　　Facilities, Services, and Activities 195
　　Hikes 196
　Two Medicine 197
　　Facilities, Services and Activities 197
　　Hikes 197
　Cut Bank 198
　　Hikes 198
　Walton 198

Hikes	199
North Fork	199
Facilities, Services, and Activities	199
Hikes	200
Goat Haunt	200
Facilities, Services, and Activities	201
Hikes	201
Last Word	202

ACKNOWLEDGEMENTS

This work would not have been possible without the support of a few very special people. I want to especially thank my dear friend Jack Tillman for all his contribution, hard work and dedication to this three book project.

I am also indebted to my brother Bobby Simms who inspired me to document my trips and start writing, who also has been supportive of my career goals and worked actively to provide me the support I needed to pursue my goals.

I am grateful to all those with whom I have had the pleasure to work with this and other related projects. Each member of my team has provided me extensive personal and professional guideline and taught me a great deal about both writing a book and publishing those works.

I would especially like to thank Denise Nicholson for her help and support in book layout, and design, without whom this monumental task would not have been done properly.

Nobody has been more important to me in the pursuit of this project than the members of my family. I would like to thank my parents, whose love and guidance are with me in whatever I pursue. They are the ultimate role models.

Most importantly, I wish to thank my loving and supportive wife Natalie, and my wonderful daughter, Liz, who always provides unending inspiration to everything I do. A special thanks to Wikipedia.org, Wikimedia.org and National Park Service for all the images and maps.

And....

To My Father, who taught me everything I know

To My Mother, without her, I won't be here

INTRODUCTION

Welcome to the second book in my three volume series all about our wonderful National Parks in our beautiful country. I hope you enjoyed reading my first book "Smart Travel Guide to 16 National Parks in the Western United States".

In this book, I am going to move on to an area known as Mountain West. This is along the Rocky Mountain Range and features a number of breathtaking rugged National Parks. In fact, this region has more of the Top 10 National Parks than any other region of the United States.

As with my first guide, I'll give you a brief overview of what you need to know of each park. This is ideal for planning your trip, or for those who already know what they want to do at a National Park and just need to learn the basics before getting started.

The second part will give you some ideas for a day trip at each park. It is all about quick tours around historical areas, a hiking trail or two— the nutshell of what you should see at that particular location in the time you have there.

Then we'll give a couple of two-week itineraries if you want a longer vacation consisting of observing hidden wildlife creatures, exploring rich landscapes, going on more strenuous walks, and seeing the flora of each location in its peak blooming point.

Finally, we'll get into the details of the National Parks that are on the Top 10 list and indulge in what is the very best of the best.

So let's get started!

PART – 1

13 NATIONAL PARKS IN THE MOUNTAIN WEST

CARLSBAD CAVERNS, NEW MEXICO

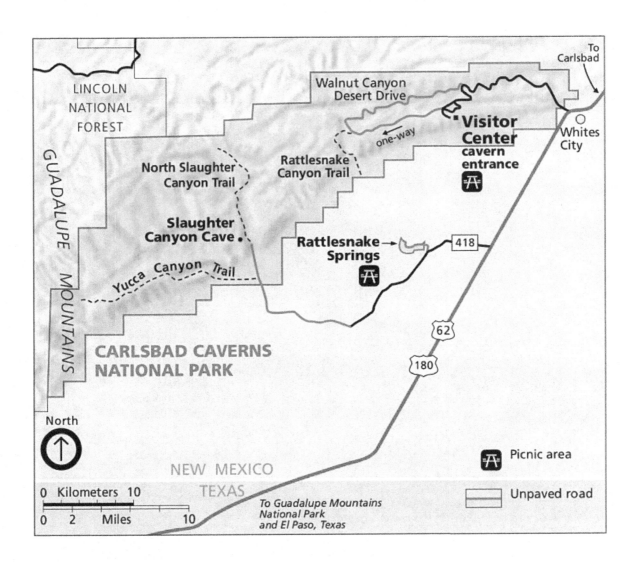

Overview

At Carlsbad Caverns National Park you'll be able to go inside some of the largest caves in North America. If you are going to vacation in New Mexico, you need to at least take a day to visit this park. On the surface, the area may not look like much, but underground there are 300 known caves, each with its own distinctive geology and history. Among these is Lechuguilla Cave, the deepest cave in the United States and the fourth largest limestone cave. Carlsbad

Caverns was given national monument status in 1923 and became a national park in 1930. Then in 1995 it became a World Heritage Site.

- **Visitor Centers / Hours**

    - The Visitor Center and Cavern have two sets of hours:

        - September 4th - May 24th

            - Visitor Center open daily, 8am to 5pm
            - Last ticket sold at 3:15pm
            - Hiking into cavern daily, 8:30am to 2:30pm
            - Last time to hike out of the cavern is 3:30pm
            - Elevator service into the cavern is from 8:30am to 3:30pm
            - Last elevator out of the cavern, 4:30pm

        - May 25th - September 2nd

            - Visitor Center open daily, 8am to 7pm
            - Last ticket sold at 4:45pm
            - Hiking into cavern daily, 8:30am to 3:30pm
            - Last time to hike out of the cavern is 5pm
            - Elevator service into the cavern is from 8:30am to 5pm
            - Last elevator out of the cavern, 6:30pm

- **Fees**

    - An entrance ticket is required and is valid for three days.

        - $12 per person over the age of 16
        - Children under 15 go in for free

- Ranger-guided tours cost extra and require reservations.

    - King's Palace: $8/adults, $4/children, senior and access pass holders. Children under four years-old are not permitted.
    - Left Hand Tunnel: $7/adults, $3.50/children, senior and access pass holders. Children under six years-old are not permitted.
    - Slaughter Canyon Cave: $15/adults, $7.50/children, senior and access pass holders. Children under eight years-old are not permitted.
    - Lower Cave: $20/adults, $10/children, senior and access pass holders. Children under 12 years of age are not permitted.
    - Hall of the White Giant: $20/adults, $10/children, senior and access pass holders. Children under 12 years of age are not permitted.
    - Spider Cave: $20/adults, $10/children, senior and access pass holders. Children under 12 years of age are not permitted.

- **Goods / Services**

    - During visitor center hours you can eat at the Carlsbad Caverns Trading Company.

- **Pets**

    - Pets are not allowed in the cavern, on park trails, off road or in the visitor center.
    - When outside your vehicle, pets must be on a leash no longer than six feet.
    - A kennel service is available for $10/day.

- **Camping**

- There is no overnight lodging or campgrounds.
- Limited primitive backcountry camping is available and requires a free permit.

- **Reservations / Permits**

    - Reservations are recommended for guided ranger tours.

- **Wildlife**

    - The deserts surrounding the cavern are home to a diverse range of mammals, birds, reptiles, and insects. The current species count includes:

        - 67 mammals, 17 species of bats
        - 357 birds
        - 55 reptiles
        - 5 fish
        - 600 insects

- **Weather**

    - Summers are hot with temperatures ranging from 90 to low 100 degrees Fahrenheit.
    - Early spring is prone to windy conditions and mild temperatures.
    - Late summer and early fall is prone to frequent rain.
    - Occasional snow and ice is possible in the winter months.

- **When to Visit**

    - The park can be visited year-round, but the best time for mild weather is in early spring.

- **Visiting Tips**
    - In the caverns, the weather is a consistent 56 degrees Fahrenheit. So equipping yourself with a light jacket may be the best option.
    - While the caverns are lighted, you may want to bring a headlamp and/or flashlight.
    - Neither food nor drinks (except for plain water) are allowed in the caverns.

ARCHES, UTAH

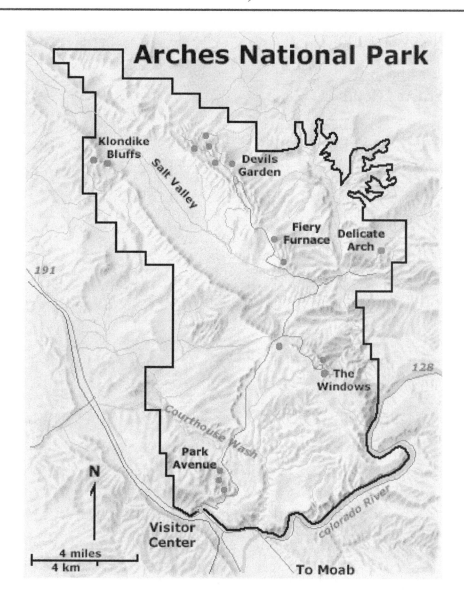

Overview

Nowhere in the world will you see as many natural sandstone arches as you will when you visit the Arches National Park in Moab, Utah. This national park includes outdoor activities such as biking, camping, rock climbing, and lots of hiking.

No matter how you want to experience this park, there is plenty to enjoy. Hikes may take a couple hours or even a half-day; there are also hikes that challenge the advanced hiker. If there is not much time for hikes, or they are not your preference, you can choose a scenic driving route to make the most out of the highlighted sights.

- **Visitor Centers / Hours**
    - The park is open 24 hours a day, year-round.
    - The Visitor Center is open daily except for December 25th.
    - The Visitor Center is open 7:30am to 5:00pm daily.

- **Fees**
    - Admission fees are good for seven days:
        - Private Vehicle - $30
        - Motorcycle - $25
        - Per Person - $15

- **Goods / Services**
    - There are no goods and services within the park, but Moab is a town five miles south of the park entrance that has full services.

- **Pets**
    - Pets are allowed, but need to be on a leash at all times and are limited in the activities they can take part in.
    - Pets are allowed in the following areas:
        - Park roads
        - Parking areas
        - Picnic areas
        - Devils Garden Campground

- Pets are not allowed in the following areas:
    - Overlooks
    - Hiking trails
    - Off trails
    - Visitor Center

- **Camping**
    - Camping is the most popular way of staying at the Arches National Park.
    - The Devils Garden Campground has 50 sites and is open year-round.

- **Reservations / Permits**
    - Reservations are required for campsites from March 1st to October 31st.
    - From November 1st to February 28th, all campsites are 'first come, first served'.

- **Wildlife**
    - Wildlife may seem scarce at first glance, but if you delve deeper into the gardens and trails, you will find there is quite the variety of creatures at Arches.
    - Birds, lizards, and some rodents are the most commonly seen wildlife in the area.
    - Most animals are nocturnal, such as kangaroo rats, foxes, mountain lions, owls, and bats.
    - Other animals you may see at dawn and dusk include:
        - Mule deer

- [ ] Coyotes
- [ ] Black-tailed jackrabbits
- [ ] Rock squirrels
- [ ] Chipmunks
- [ ] Eagles

- [ ] **Weather**

    - [ ] Spring and fall offer comfortable temperatures and are the best seasons to plan your visit.
    - [ ] Summer has intense daytime temperatures that can often be over 100 degrees Fahrenheit.
    - [ ] Winter doesn't have as many crowds, but temperatures often stay between 30 and 50 degrees Fahrenheit.

- [ ] **When to Visit**

    - [ ] The park can be visited year-round, the busiest times are March through October.

- [ ] **Visiting Tips**

    - [ ] It is best to get an early start to beat both crowds and heat.
    - [ ] There is little shade, so extreme heat is possible in the warmer months. Always bring a hat and sunglasses, plus plenty of water.
    - [ ] In colder months, dress in layers.

BRYCE CANYON, UTAH

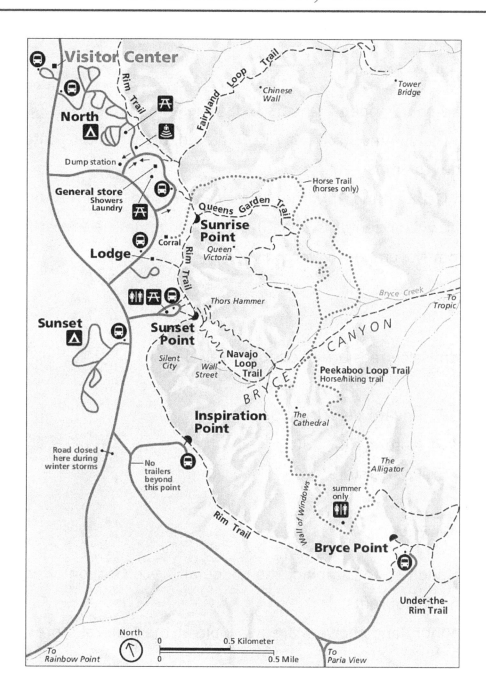

Overview

At Bryce Canyon National Park you will see beautiful carved rock formations and breathtaking vistas. There are numerous outdoor activities to enjoy, plus three unique climate zones.

The area was first designated a National Monument in 1923 and then became established as a National Park in 1928.

- **Visitor Centers / Hours**
  - The park is open 24 hours a day, year-round.
  - In the summer from May to September, the visitor center is open 8am to 8pm.
  - In October and April the visitor center is open 8am to 6pm.
  - The visitor center is open 8am to 4:30pm in the winter months, or from November to March.

- **Fees**
  - Admission fees are good for seven days:
    - Private Vehicle - $35
    - Motorcycle - $30
    - Per Person - $20

- **Goods / Services**
  - In addition to camping, the Lodge at Bryce Canyon offers lodging and restaurants.
  - Laundry and showers are available at the general store.

- **Pets**
  - Pets must be on a leash no longer than six feet and are only permitted in the following areas:
    - Campgrounds
    - Parking lots

- ☐ Paved roads
- ☐ Paved viewpoint areas
- ☐ Paved trails

- ☐ **Camping**
    - ☐ There are two reservation-based car camping sites.
    - ☐ You can also camp at multiple sites along the trails with a backcountry camping permit.

- ☐ **Reservations / Permits**
    - ☐ Reservations are recommended for camping and lodging.

- ☐ **Wildlife**
    - ☐ The biodiversity of the various ecosystems in the National Park is home to over 100 species of birds and dozens of mammals.

- ☐ **Weather**
    - ☐ The sky is sunny most the year, but the temperatures can be unpredictable for the most part.
    - ☐ Thunderstorms are an almost daily occurrence in the summer, and large snowstorms aren't uncommon in the winter.

- ☐ **When to Visit**
    - ☐ The park can be visited year-round.

- ☐ **Visiting Tips**
    - ☐ Dehydration is an issue at this park due to its altitude and dry desert air. Plan and pack for enough water and proper supplies.

- ☐ The only outdoor activity not allowed in Bryce Canyon is mountain biking.

CANYONLANDS, UTAH

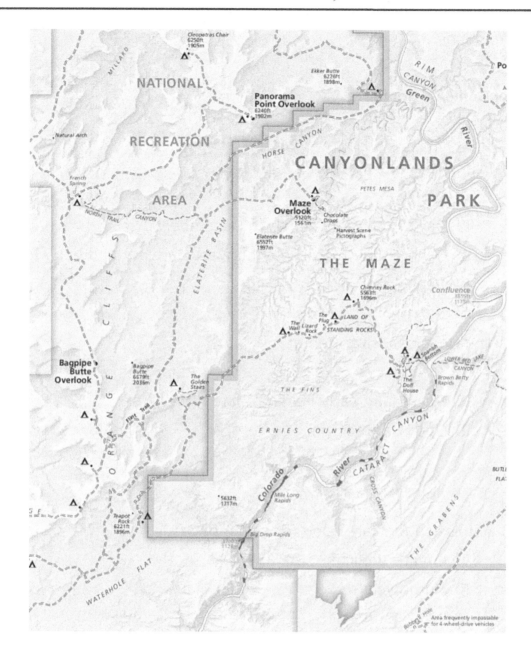

Overview

Canyonlands National Park is located along the powerful Colorado River. You can enjoy everything from hiking to technical rock climbing here. Established as a National Park in 1964, Canyonlands offers 527 square miles of canyons, mesas, arches, and buttes along the Colorado River.

The park is divided into four districts: the Island in the Sky, the Needles, the Maze, and the Rivers. Each of these places has its own character and exploration options.

- **Visitor Centers / Hours**
    - The park is open 24 hours a day, year-round.
    - Island in the Sky Visitor Center
        - Daily from early March to December
        - Open Friday to Tuesday between January and early March
        - Open 8am to 6pm
    - The Needles Visitor Center
        - Open daily early March to late November
        - Open 8am to 5pm

- **Fees**
    - Admission fees are good for seven days:
        - Private Vehicle - $30
        - Motorcycle - $25
        - Per Person - $15

- **Goods / Services**
    - There aren't any services in the park, so you'll need to bring what you need. Nearby towns offer full services.

- **Pets**

- Pets must be on a leash no longer than six feet and are only permitted in the following areas:

    - Campgrounds
    - Parking lots
    - Paved roads

- **Camping**

    - There are two campground options in Canyonlands National Park:

        - Willow Flat Campground at Island in the Sky

            - 12 sites open year-round
            - First come, first served
            - Toilets, picnic tables, and fire rings. No water service.
            - $15 per night

        - Squaw Flat Campground at The Needles

            - 26 individual sites and three group sites
            - Some sites are reserved in spring and fall, while the others are first come, first served.
            - Toilets, picnic tables, and fire rings are also available
            - $20 per night

- **Reservations / Permits**

    - Some campsites at Squaw Flat Campground will require reservations in the spring and fall.

- **Wildlife**

- Birds, lizards, and some rodents are the most commonly seen.

- **Weather**
    - Summers are extremely hot and winters are very cold.
    - There is less than 10 inches of rainfall a year.
    - Temperatures can vary as much as 50 degrees in a single day.

- **When to Visit**
    - The park can be visited year-round.

- **Visiting Tips**
    - It is best to wear loose-fitting, light-colored clothing that covers your body. A hat is highly recommended.
    - It is recommended to drink at least a gallon of water a day.
    - Leave strenuous activities for the early morning or early evening hours, especially in the summer when temperatures are over 100 degrees Fahrenheit.
    - Consider visiting in a four-wheel-drive vehicle since many of the roads in the remote areas of the park travel over rugged terrain.
    - Fuel up before arriving– the nearest services are 50 miles away.

CAPITOL REEF, UTAH

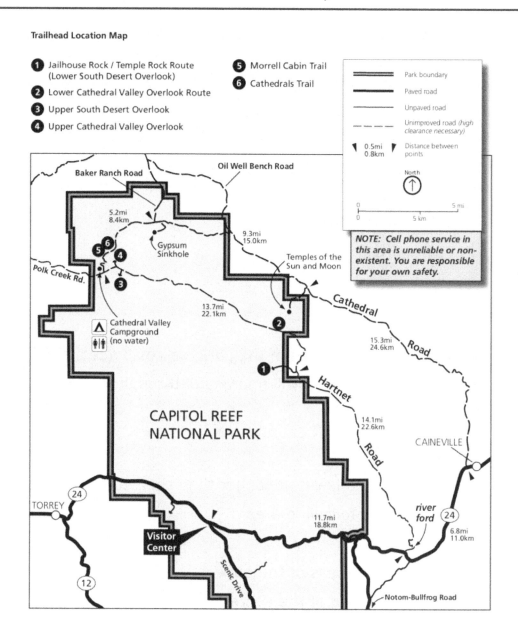

Overview

The Capitol Reef National Park in Utah features nearly a quarter million acres of habitats going from pinyon-juniper, streams, dry washes, and rock cliffs. You'll find a diverse variety of plant and animal life to observe or photograph as well.

- **Visitor Centers / Hours**

- The park is open 24 hours a day, year-round.
- The visitor center is open daily, except for some major holidays from 8am to 4:30pm.

- **Fees**
    - Admission fees are valid for seven days:
        - Private Vehicle - $15
        - Motorcycle - $10
        - Per Person - $7

- **Goods / Services**
    - There aren't any services in the park, so you'll need to bring every piece of equipment you will find useful throughout your trip.

- **Pets**
    - Pets must be on a leash no longer than six feet and are only permitted in the following areas:
        - Developed areas of the park
        - Within 50 feet of the centerline of public vehicle roads, both paved and dirt.
        - Unfenced and/or unlocked orchards
        - Picnic areas
        - Campgrounds

- **Camping**
    - Fruita Campground is the only developed campground in the park with 71 sites.

- ☐ Cedar Mesa and Cathedral are primitive campgrounds in remote areas of the park.

☐ **Reservations / Permits**

- ☐ Reservations are needed for group campsites.
- ☐ A free permit is needed for backcountry camping and hiking.

☐ **Wildlife**

- ☐ There is a diverse range of wildlife to view in the area, mostly involving animals that are scavengers such as small rodents and several species of birds and reptiles.

☐ **Weather**

- ☐ The park has a very arid climate with under 10 inches of rain a year.

☐ **When to Visit**

- ☐ The park can be visited year-round.

☐ **Visiting Tips**

- ☐ It is important to wear a hat and sunglasses while drinking plenty of water to avoid dehydration.
- ☐ If you are visiting in July be sure to stop by the orchards of Fruita and pick fruit from the trees for free.

ZION NATIONAL PARK, UTAH

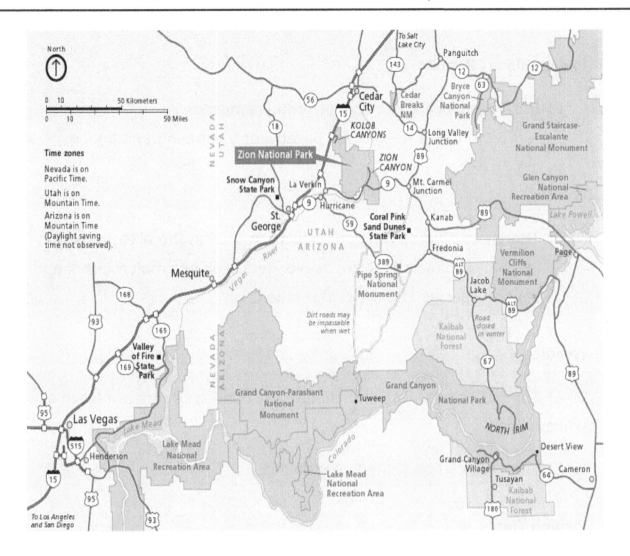

Overview

Zion National Park offers a outdoor activities in each of its geographic regions. It was originally named Mukuntuweap National Monument in 1909, and was granted national park status in 1919. The highlight of the park is an extensive canyon system with both easy hikes and more challenging ones for the avid hiker.

- **Visitor Centers / Hours**
    - The park is open 24 hours a day, year-round.

- Zion Canyon Visitor Center

    - May 3 to May 25, 8am to 6pm
    - May 26 to September 3, 8am to 7pm
    - September 4 to October 8, 8am to 6pm

- Kolob Canyons Visitor Center closed until October 1st

- **Fees**

    - Admission fees are valid for seven days:

        - Private Vehicle - $35
        - Motorcycle - $30
        - Per Person - $20

- **Goods / Services**

    - Water refilling stations are located throughout the main canyon as well as the following areas:

        - Visitor Center
        - Zion Human History Museum
        - Zion Lodge
        - The Grotto
        - Temple of Sinawava

    - Zion Lodge offers year-round lodging and a post office.
    - The Red Rock Grill Dining Room and Castle Dome Cafe are available at the Zion Lodge.

- **Pets**

- Pets must be on a leash no longer than six feet and are only permitted on the Pa'rus Trail.

- **Camping**
    - Camping is available at three campgrounds:
        - South Campground
        - Watchman Campground
        - Lava Point Campground

- **Reservations / Permits**
    - Reservations can be made for South and Watchman Campground through www.recreation.gov

- **Wildlife**
    - Commonly seen wildlife include lizards, mule deer, and wild turkeys.
    - Keep your eye out for dangerous animals such as mountain lions and rattlesnakes. Remember to stay in the safe trails marked by rangers, do not leave any food out in the open air, and never approach those creatures (if you see them, it means you are the intruder in their territory, and they are more than capable of defending their land through very violent ways).

- **Weather**
    - In the summer, temperatures can reach over 100 degrees Fahrenheit on the canyon floor, and 90 degrees Fahrenheit or more at higher elevations.
    - Flash flooding from thunderstorms is common in summer months.
    - Spring and fall offer warm days and cool nights.
    - Snowstorms can happen in late spring and early summer.
    - In winter, temperatures can drop to below freezing in the nighttime.

- **When to Visit**
    - The park can be visited year-round, but spring and fall offer the most comfortable weather.

- **Visiting Tips**
    - As with visiting other desert environments, make sure you drink plenty of water. It is best to drink at least a gallon per person, per day. Make it a point to wear protective gear and carry a lighter bag.

ROCKY MOUNTAIN, COLORADO

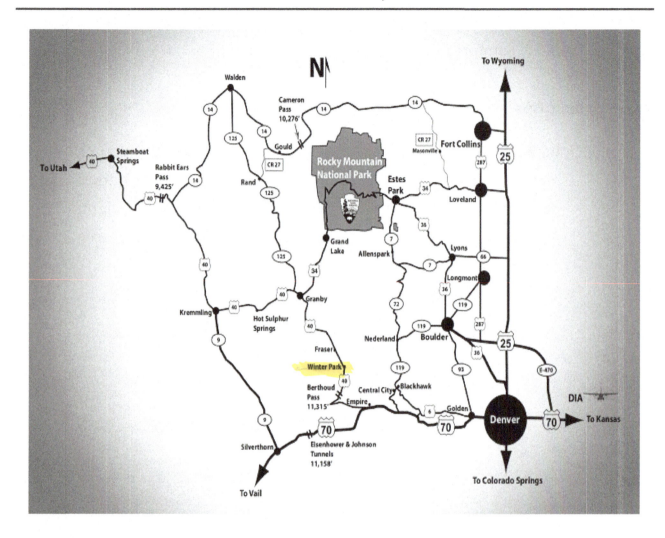

Overview

Established in 1915, there is no better way to experience the Rocky Mountains than at the Rocky Mountain National Park. This is a great destination for families and individuals with a glorious array of activities in a beautiful, majestic mountain setting.

- **Visitor Centers / Hours**
    - The park is open 24 hours a day, year-round.
    - Beaver Meadows Visitor Center

- May 15 to June 18, open daily 8am to 5pm
- November 5 to May 26, open daily 9am to 4:30pm
- Closed December 25th and Thanksgiving

- Alpine Visitor Center

  - Closed from October 10 to May 26
  - Open daily for the rest of the year from 9am to 5pm

- Fall River Visitor Center

  - Closed from November 5 to May 26 with the following exceptions:
    - Open 9am to 4pm on November 25th and 27th, and December 3-4, 10-11, 17-18, 19-24, 26-January 1st.
  - October 1st to October 9 open daily 9am to 4pm
  - Open daily 9am to 5pm throughout the rest of the year

- Kawuneeche Visitor Center

  - September 4th to 30th open daily 8am to 5pm
  - Open daily from 8am to 6pm for the rest of the year
  - Closed December 25th and Thanksgiving

- **Fees**

  - Admission fees are valid for seven days:

    - Private Vehicle - $35
    - Motorcycle - $30
    - Per Person - $20

- ☐ A single day pass is $30 per vehicle
- ☐ A annual pass is available for $70

☐ **Goods / Services**

- ☐ There are limited services within the park:
    - ☐ From late May to early October the Trail Ridge Store offers a cafe.
    - ☐ The Rocky Mountain Conservancy offers limited food items.

☐ **Pets**

- ☐ Pets must be on a leash no longer than six feet and are only allowed in the following areas:
    - ☐ Established roads
    - ☐ Parking areas
    - ☐ Campgrounds
    - ☐ Picnic Areas

☐ **Camping**

- ☐ Camping is available at five established campgrounds.
- ☐ There are also many backcountry areas for camping.

☐ **Reservations / Permits**

- ☐ Reservations can be made for some campgrounds through www.recreation.gov

☐ **Wildlife**

- ☐ Drive through the park at dusk and you are likely to see herds of elk and mule deer.
- ☐ The area is also a prime spot for viewing the following:

    - ☐ Moose
    - ☐ Bighorn Sheep
    - ☐ Black Bears
    - ☐ Coyotes
    - ☐ Cougars
    - ☐ Eagles
    - ☐ Hawks
    - ☐ Pikas
    - ☐ Marmots

- ☐ **Weather**

    - ☐ The weather can be extreme and unpredictable.
    - ☐ Snowstorms are common in winter.
    - ☐ Summer is short and only lasts from July through August, but reaches temperatures of 80 degrees Fahrenheit in the day and 40 degrees at night.
    - ☐ Snow can be expected at most elevations year-round.
    - ☐ Lightning storms are common in summer afternoons. Wear rubber and stay away from metallic equipment.

- ☐ **When to Visit**

- ☐ Autumn is a beautiful time to visit, and June and July offer peak wildflower-viewing.

- ☐ **Visiting Tips**

- ☐ It is best to get an early start at about 6am in order to avoid crowds and afternoon thunderstorms.
- ☐ Trail Ridge Road is the main road through the park, but can be clogged with traffic, so you will want to consider other roads if you want to hike the wilderness.
- ☐ You should do your reservations at least three months in advance.
- ☐ You can legally enter the park for free from the Longs Peak and St. Vrain trailheads.

MESA VERDE, COLORADO

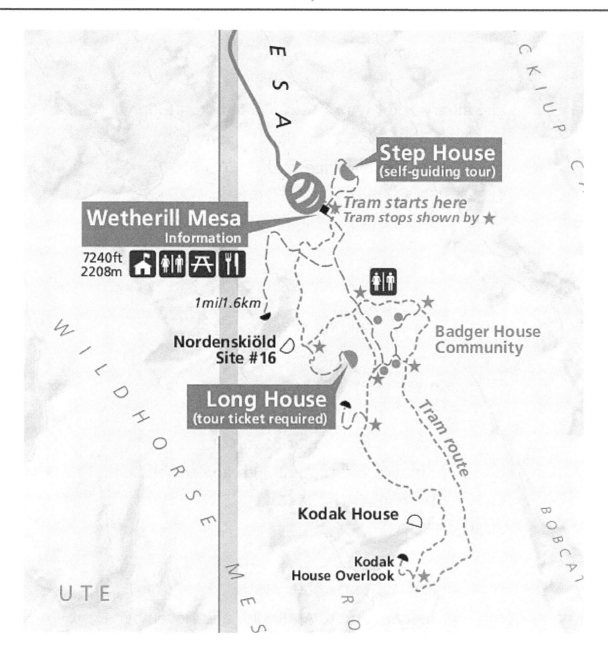

Overview

In Spanish, Mesa Verde is literally translated to "Green Table" and this is certainly what this national park's unique landscape resembles. Mesa Verde National Park is home to over 4,000 archeological sites that date as far back as A.D. 550. The ancient cliff dwellings here are among the most noted and best preserved in the United States.

- **Visitor Centers / Hours**

    - The park is open 24 hours a day, year-round.
    - Visitor Center Hours:

        - January 2nd to April 14th, 8:30am to 4:30pm
        - April 15th to May 24th, 8am to 5pm
        - May 25th to September 3rd, 7:30am to 7pm
        - September 4th to October 20th, 8am to 5pm
        - October 21th to December 31st, 8:30am to 4:30pm

- **Fees**

    - Admission fees are valid for seven days:

        - Private Vehicle

            - May 1st to October 31st, $20
            - January 2nd to April 30th and November 1st to December 31st, $15
        - Motorcycles

            - May 1st to October 31st, $15
            - January 2nd to April 30th and November 1st to December 31st, $10
        - Per Person

            - May 1st to October 31st, $10
            - January 2nd to April 30th and November 1st to December 31st, $7
        - An annual pass is available for $40

- **Goods / Services**
  - In addition to camping, you can stay at the Far View Lodge.
  - At the Far View Lodge you have the following dining options:
    - Metate Room Restaurant
    - Far View Lounge
    - Far View Terrace Café
  - Other dining locations in the park include Spruce Tree Terrace Cafe and Wetherill Mesa Snack Bar.
  - Hours for these services vary, so check before visiting.

- **Pets**
  - Pets must be on a leash no longer than six feet and are only allowed in the following areas:
    - Paved roads
    - Parking lots
    - Campgrounds

- **Camping**
  - Camping is available at Morefield Campground.
  - It is available April 19th to October 17th, with limited services the rest of the year.
  - Even though there are 267 sites, reservations are still recommended.

- **Reservations / Permits**
  - Both camping and lodging require reservations through Aramark.

- **Wildlife**
    - The park is home to a wide range of wildlife including:
        - 74 mammals
        - 200 birds
        - 16 reptiles
        - 5 amphibians
        - 6 fish
        - 1,000+ insects

- **Weather**
    - The weather is fairly pleasant year-round.
    - Snowstorms are still possible in the winter, and the summer can be dry and hot. For the most part, the temperature stays at the same level– a middle ground that has warm sun, but still fairly cool winds.

- **When to Visit**
    - You can visit year-round and but May to October offer you the most viewing and camping opportunities.

- **Visiting Tips**
    - Always check the park website before you go since cliff dwellings and other specific sections may be closed at any time due to loose rocks, poor weather, and/or repairs.
    - There are wild horses in the park so always drive slowly and carefully. Avoid making direct contact with the horses and please do not feed them, since not only will it be dangerous for you (territory-wise), but also because they are already used to acquiring their

nutrients from their natural surroundings, and anything out of those surroundings may be harmful to their digestive system

GREAT SAND DUNES, COLORADO

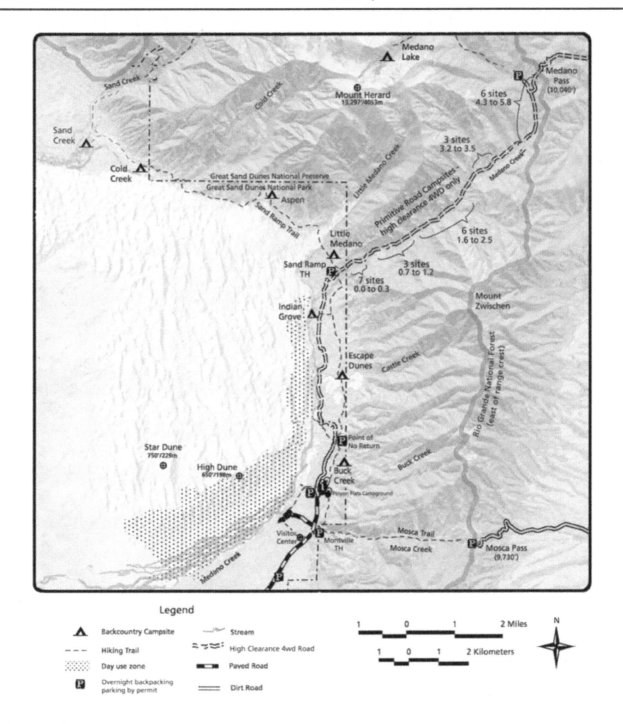

Overview

Southern Colorado may seem like an unlikely location for a national park featuring the tallest dunes in North America, but this rugged destination features the Sangre de Cristo Mountains standing at over 750 feet high. This area became a national monument in 1932 and was later named a national park and preserve.

- **Visitor Centers / Hours**

    - The park is open 24 hours a day, year-round.
    - Visitor Center Hours:

        - Memorial Day to Labor Day, 8:30am to 5pm
        - Labor Day to Memorial Day, 9am to 4:30pm

- **Fees**

    - Admission fees are valid for seven days:

        - Private Vehicle $20
        - Motorcycle $15
        - An annual pass is available for $40

- **Goods / Services**

    - In addition to camping, there are four lodging options:

        - Great Sand Dunes Lodge
        - Oasis Camping Cabins
        - Oasis Duplex Motel
        - Zapata Ranch
        - You should contact each of these facilities for operating hours and rates.

    - The only restaurant in the park is the Oasis Restaurant and Store at the park entrance. It is open April through October.

- In addition to the Oasis, general supplies can be found at the Mosca Pass Outpost in the Piñon Flats Campground.

- **Pets**

    - Pets must be on a leash no longer than six feet and are only allowed in the following areas:
        - All areas of the Preserve including Mosca Pass Trail
        - Main use areas of the park

- **Camping**

    - Camping is available at Piñon Flats Campground
    - Open April through October

- **Reservations / Permits**

    - All campsites can be reserved through www.recreation.gov

- **Wildlife**

    - The park offers an abundance of wildlife.
    - Beware of black bears and mountains lions.

- **Weather**

    - March and April tend to have snow days intermixed with warm days. Spring can also bring high winds in the afternoon.
    - In the summer, sandy areas can easily reach temperatures over 150 degrees Fahrenheit on the surface. However, even warm clothing is recommended for the summer evenings.
    - Fall is a time for mainly mild weather in the park, but still come prepared for anything.

- Winter offers very cold weather than can sometimes dip below zero degrees Fahrenheit with occasional blizzards.

- **When to Visit**

    - Even though you can visit the park year-round, from a weather standpoint, the fall is the most favorable time to plan your trip.

- **Visiting Tips**

    - The surrounding areas of the national park are very windy, so make sure you bring eye protection (sunglasses) and a handkerchief or bandana to protect your face in case of really strong winds.
    - If you are traveling in the summer be prepared to hike in the early morning and later evening to avoid the hot sand. It is always a great idea to visit during weekdays when there are less crowds.
    - If traveling in June, come prepared for a large amount of mosquitos along Medano Creek.

BLACK CANYON OF THE GUNNISON, COLORADO

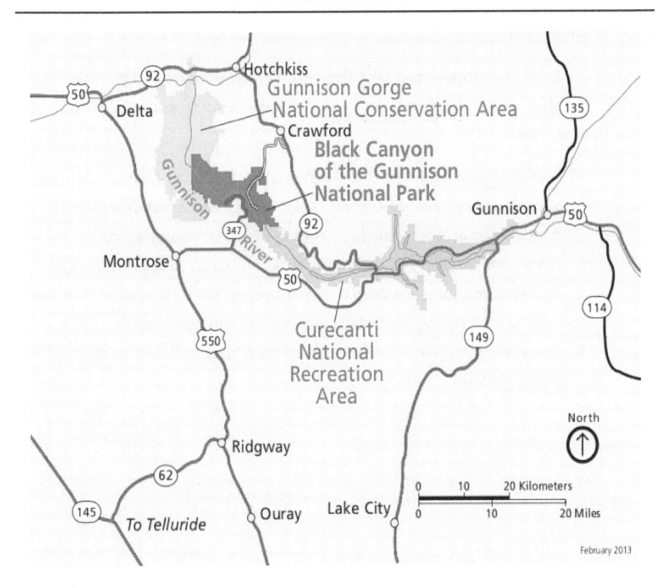

Overview

For the outdoor enthusiasts, Black Canyon offers excellent experiences, from technical rock climbing to backwoods hiking adventures.

No other canyon in North America compares to those you find at this national park. Do your research and come prepared, since most activities are strenuous and somewhat dangerous.

- **Visitor Centers / Hours**
    - The South Rim of the park is open all the time.
    - The North Rim is closed from November to April.
    - The Visitor Center is located on the South Rim

        - Closed Thanksgiving and Christmas Day
        - September 4th to October 27th, 8am to 5pm
        - October 28th to April 13th, 9am to 4pm
        - April 14th to May 23rd, 8am to 5pm
        - May 24th to Labor Day, 8am to 6pm

- **Fees**
    - Admission fees are valid for seven days:

        - Private Vehicle $20
        - Motorcycle $15
        - Individuals $10
        - An annual pass is available for $40

- **Goods / Services**
    - There are no goods and services available in the park, so nearby towns are the best option.

- **Pets**
    - Pets must be on a leash no longer than six feet and are only allowed in the following areas:

        - Roads
        - North Rim Campground

- [ ] To the overlooks
- [ ] Cedar Point Nature Trail
- [ ] North Rim Chasm View Nature Trail

- [ ] From June 1st to August 10th, dogs are allowed in South Rim campsites, but are not permitted to travel around the campground due to aggressive deer protecting their fawns.

- [ ] **Camping**

    - [ ] Camping is available at three campgrounds:

        - [ ] North Rim
        - [ ] South Rim
        - [ ] East Portal

    - [ ] South Rim campsites can be reserved while the rest are first come, first served.

- [ ] **Reservations / Permits**

    - [ ] Campsites can be reserved through www.recreation.gov

- [ ] **Wildlife**

    - [ ] The predominant wildlife consists of singing wrens, eagles, magpies, coyotes, elk, and an abundant amount of mule deer herds.

- [ ] **Weather**

    - [ ] The park experiences the four standard seasons, so come prepared for fresh springs surrounded by wildflowers still in their buds, warm summers in full bloom, windy falls with dry leaves, and cold winters with snow.

- **When to Visit**
    - The park can be visited year-round, but is limited by snow in the winter months. So, the best times to visit are spring or summer.

- **Visiting Tips**
    - Ensure you check and plan your trip in advance; pack appropriate gear and supplies.
    - Day-use permits are limited and you may not get into the park if you arrive late on busy weekends.

YELLOWSTONE
IDAHO/MONTANA/WYOMING

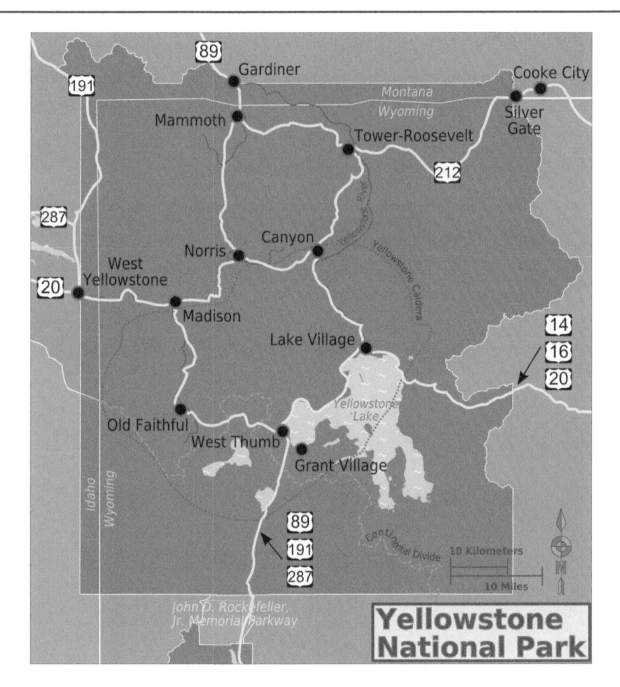

Overview

There is no other national park like Yellowstone and the many activities it offers for people of all types and preferences. This park was established in 1872 and is largely in Wyoming, but also extends into parts of Idaho and Montana. It was the first national park in the United States and today stands as one of the most popular and largest.

The focus of Yellowstone is the dormant volcano, surrounding geysers, and hot springs that are more abundant than any other place on earth. Old Faithful geyser at this park is one of the most famous natural wonders in the United States, affectionately nicknamed for its predictable, punctual explosions.

- **Visitor Centers / Hours**
    - Albright Visitor Center
        - September 4th to June 19th, 9am to 5pm
        - Rest of the year, 8am to 6pm
    - Canyon Visitor Education Center
        - Closed November 5th to April 19th
        - Summer, 8am to 6pm
        - Rest of the time, 9am to 5pm
    - Fishing Bridge Visitor Center
        - Open late May to early September, 8am to 7pm
    - Grant Visitor Center
        - Open late May to early October, 8am to 7pm
- **Fees**
    - Admission fees are valid for seven days:

- Private Vehicle $35
- Motorcycle $30
- Individuals $20
- An annual pass is available for $70

- **Goods / Services**

    - Yellowstone offers a wide range of services to help you get the most out of your time at the park.
    - Medical services are available at three clinics:

        - Mammoth Clinic open year-round
        - Lake Clinic and Old Faithful Clinic open in the summer

    - Post Offices are located at:

        - Canyon Village
        - Grant Village
        - Lake Village
        - Mammoth Hot Springs
        - Old Faithful

    - Service Stations are located at:

        - Canyon Village
        - Fishing Bridge
        - Grant Village
        - Mammoth Hot Springs
        - Old Faithful
        - Tower Junction

- There are a total of nine lodges within Yellowstone that offer over 2,000 rooms. They are open late spring through fall. Only Old Faithful Snow Lodge and Mammoth Hot Springs Hotel are open in the winter.
- There is no shortage of dining options throughout the park such as fine dining to snack bars and cafeterias. Find out about your nearby locations and their menus at your lodge or at a visitor center.
- There are also several general stores throughout the park that allow you to buy all the supplies you need for your stay.

- **Pets**
  - Pets must be on a leash no longer than six feet and are only allowed in the following areas:
    - Developed areas within 100 feet of roads, parking areas, and campgrounds.
- **Camping**
  - Camping is available at 12 campgrounds with over 2,000 sites.

- **Reservations / Permits**
  - All lodges and <u>five of the campgrounds require reservations</u> through Yellowstone National Park Lodges.
- **Wildlife**
  - Yellowstone is home to the largest and oldest bison herd.
  - Other mammals include wolves, elk, and grizzly bears.

- **Weather**
  - The elevation of the park leads to a dramatic difference in weather from day to day.

- ☐ Snow in the summer and temperatures of 80 degrees Fahrenheit in the fall are possible.
- ☐ Always pack and wear layered clothing to prepare yourself for any type of weather.

☐ **When to Visit**

- ☐ The park can be visited year-round.

☐ **Visiting Tips**

- ☐ There are three main wildlife regions where you can spot dozens of animals. The best times to catch a glimpse of them is just right after sunrise.
- ☐ Drive slowly and carefully because of the abundance of wildlife that may appear on the main roads. Accidentally running over a deer or any type of animal at a national park with a car is not only traumatizing, but also expensive.
- ☐ Even if you don't stay in a lodge, take the time to visit one and enjoy the architecture.

GRAND TETON, WYOMING

Death Canyon Trailhead

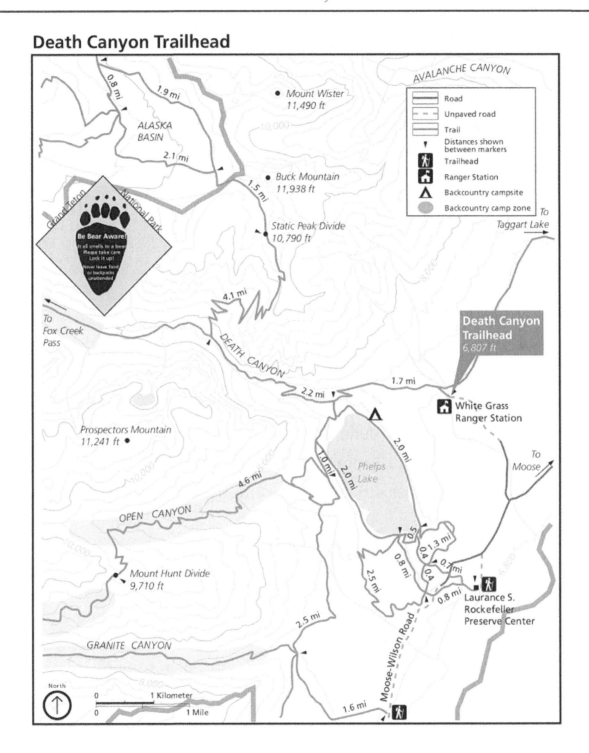

Overview

Grand Teton National Park was established in 1929 and extended into the surrounding valley in 1950. The 310,000 acres of this park feature a diverse ecosystem and wildlife, as well as dozens of outdoor activities you can participate in during your stay.

- **Visitor Centers / Hours**
    - The park is open year-round, but there are some road closures in the winter months.
    - Craig Thomas Discovery and Visitor Center
        - March 5th to April 30th, 10am to 4pm
        - May 1st to June 5th, 8am to 5pm
        - June 6th to September 22nd, 8am to 7pm
        - September 23th to October 31st, 8am to 5pm
    - Colter Bay Visitor Center
        - May 11th to June 5th, 8am to 5pm
        - June 6th to September 3rd, 8am to 7pm
        - September 4th to October 8th, 8am to 5pm
    - Jenny Lake Visitor Center
        - May 18th to June 5th, 8am to 5pm
        - June 6th to September 3th, 8am to 7pm
        - September 4th to September 23rd, 8am to 5pm
- **Fees**
    - Admission fees are valid for seven days:
        - Private Vehicle $35
        - Motorcycle $30

- Individuals $20
- An annual pass is available for $70

- **Goods / Services**
    - There are limited services in the park, but there are plenty of lodging options for those who don't want to camp. You can stay in a modern motel or lodge or you can stay at a rustic cabin.

- **Pets**
    - Pets must be on a leash no longer than six feet and are only allowed in the following areas:
        - Pets must stay within 30 feet of any roadway.

- **Camping**
    - Camping is available at five campgrounds.

- **Reservations / Permits**
    - Most campgrounds are first come, first served, but you will need reservations for group camping.

- **Wildlife**
    - Larger mammal species include grizzly and black bears, wolves, coyotes, bison, and bald eagles.
    - There is also a wide variety of smaller species as well.

- **Weather**
    - The park is covered in snow from November to May. Although snow can occasionally fall in May and June as well.

- In the summer, thunderstorms and rain aren't uncommon.

- **When to Visit**

    - The park can be visited year-round. But come prepared for sub-zero temperatures if you come in winter.

- **Visiting Tips**

    - Drive slowly and carefully because of the abundance of wildlife.
    - Come prepared for cooler weather, even during the warmer months.

GLACIER, MONTANA

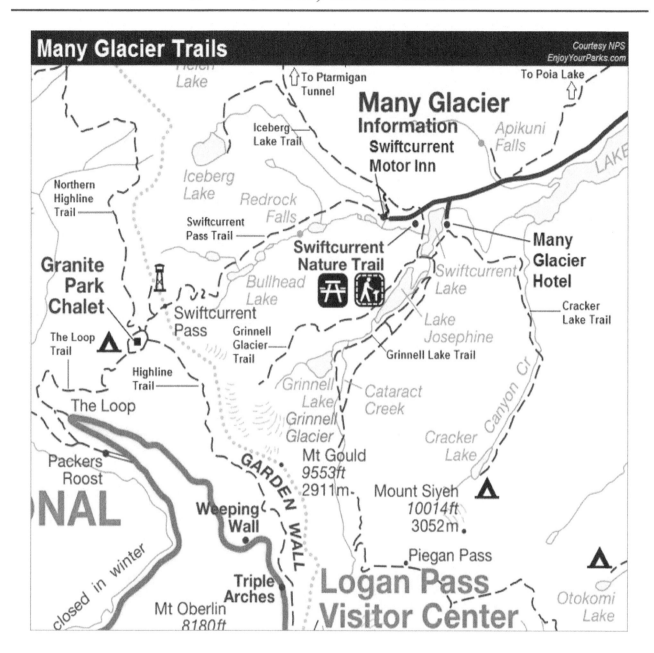

Overview

Established in 1910, Glacier National Park includes about a million acres of land and 25 active glaciers. There is plenty to see and do to enjoy the great outdoors at this park. There are even some remote areas where you can enjoy a true wilderness experience.

- **Visitor Centers / Hours**
    - The park is open year-round, but most facilities aren't open in the winter months.
    - Apgar Visitor Center
        - January to May 12th open weekends only, 9am to 4:30pm
        - May 13th to June 9th open daily 9am to 4:30pm
        - June 10th to September 4th open daily 8am to 6pm
        - September 5th to October 9th open day 8am to 5pm
        - October 10th to November 5th open weekends only
        - November 6th closes for the rest of the year
    - Logan Pass Visitor Center
        - June 18th to September 4th open daily 9am to 7pm
        - September 5th to September 30th open daily 9:30am to 4pm
        - October 1st closes for the rest of the year
    - St. Mary Visitor Center
        - May 26th to June 17th open daily 8am to 5pm
        - June 18th to August 12th open daily 8am to 6pm
        - August 13th to September 30th open daily 8am to 5pm
        - October 1st to October 8th open daily 9am to 5pm
        - October 9th closes for the rest of the year
- **Fees**
    - Admission fees are valid for seven days:
        - Private Vehicle $35
        - Motorcycle $30

- Individuals $20
- An annual pass is available for $70

- **Goods / Services**
    - There are several lodging options in the park aside from camping. Otherwise, there are limited services within the park.

- **Pets**
    - Pets must be on a leash no longer than six feet and are only allowed in the following areas:
        - Developed areas
        - Frontcountry campgrounds
        - Picnic areas
        - Along roads
        - Parking areas
        - Boats on the lake

- **Camping**
    - Camping is available at 13 campgrounds with over 1,000 campsites.

- **Reservations / Permits**
    - Most campgrounds are first come, first served, but you will need prior reservations for some campgrounds and lodges.

- **Wildlife**
    - There are dozens of mammal species including mountain goats, wolves, grizzly bears, and wolverines. Needless to say, if you see any of these creatures, never feed them, and do not approach them

if you can help it, as they may be either defending their territory or their kin.
- In addition there are over 300 species of birds including the golden eagle.

- **Weather**
    - Weather varies greatly throughout the year.
    - Temperatures can be as high as 90 degrees Fahrenheit in the summer and as low as 20 degrees Fahrenheit in winter.
    - The east side is sunny while the west side tends to be rainy.

- **When to Visit**
    - The park can be visited year-round.
    - Summer and spring tend to be the best times to visit.

- **Visiting Tips**
    - If visiting in the summer, you can take a free shuttle around the park in order to peacefully bask in the more tourist-destination sights.
    - If you want to travel the backcountry, you should apply for a permit in mid-March.

PART -2

WHAT TO SEE AND DO IN A DAY TRIP

CARLSBAD CAVERNS, NEW MEXICO

There are two ways to explore Carlsbad Caverns if you are taking a day trip there. You can choose one of two self-guided tours or you can take a ranger-led tour. Let's first consider your options for a self-guided tour.

The two self-guided tours are The Big Room and Natural Entrance. Each of these are 1.25-mile trails that provide you with unique experiences. You can likely do both tours in a single day with plenty of time to spare afterward.

The Big Room is a huge room the size of six football fields. The hike is very mild with mostly flat ground. You'll be able to see a variety of rock formations. You can reach this trail through an elevator in the visitor center, and it is ideal for those using a wheelchair or who are traveling with small children.

The Natural Entrance Trail is accessed by a steep 750-foot descent that can be a bit strenuous for some. However, this path takes you in the footsteps of the original explorers of the cave, as well as some of the more famous formations. You can also choose to bypass the elevator lines and hike back out through this trail.

If you still have time in your day or if you choose to forgo the self-guided tours, consider taking one of the many ranger-guided tours available. The best and most recommended ranger tour is the King's Palace, which will lead you into the deepest portion of the cavern at 830 feet beneath the desert.

If you spend the entire day there, do stay to see the nightly bat exodus. From May to mid-October, hundreds of thousands of bats fill the sky as they leave the cave in the evening. The best times to view the bat flights is in July and August when the pups fly for the first time. You can also watch the pre-dawn return in the morning if you're more of an early riser.

While the main focus of this national park is to view the underground caverns, there is still a lot of see and enjoy above ground. In fact, it can be an excellent option if you prefer solitude away from the crowds. A great option is the half-mile Desert Nature Walk– found near the Visitor's Center– that gives you a chance to view multitudes of wildflowers in bloom.

Another good day hike option is the Rattlesnake Canyon Trail. This is a six-mile out-and-back trail that moderately descends into a side ravine to a rocky wash and takes you by an old homestead. You can access the trail from the nine-mile marker on Walnut Canyon Desert Drive.

If you prefer a more strenuous and wilderness hike then there are two ranger-led hikes to consider. The first is the Slaughter Canyon tour that starts at the Visitor's Center. You start with a strenuous 30-45 minute hike uphill to the cavern entrance. This tour will last about five and a half hours.

There is also the ranger-led Spider Cave tour. This is a 3D-maze cave with a lot of climbing and crawling. It starts with a half-mile hike down into the canyon to reach the cave entrance. Now, the Spider Cave tour is not a good idea for those afraid of tight spaces or heights.

ARCHES, UTAH

If you only have a day when visiting Arches National Park in Utah there are two ways you can explore the park and still get a worthwhile visit. You can choose to tour the park by car or by taking a day hike.

VIEWING THE PARK BY CAR

In an hour and a half you can do one of two drives:

1. Drive to the Windows Section to view some of the largest arches in the park.

2. Drive to the Delicate Arch Viewpoint to see the most famous arch from a distance. On your way back, you can stop at Wolfe Ranch to witness what homesteading was like in the late 1800s in the region.

For a longer route, you can take three hours to drive the whole park road and have 10-minute pit stops at each viewpoint along the way.

If you have at least half a day to spend, you can go on a short walk at the Windows Section, Delicate Arch Viewpoint, and/or Balanced Rock to get a little closer to the landscape.

DAY HIKES IN THE PARK

If you have limited time at the park, there are four short hikes you can choose from that last about two hours each:

1. The Windows Loop trail takes you between the parking area and Double Arch. On the way back, you can hike to Balanced Rock and walk around the base.
2. You can also hike up to see Delicate Arch. However, it is best to avoid hiking this trail during midday in summer.
3. Walk between the fins of Devils Garden to view the Landscape Arch, the longest arch in North America.
4. Hike the trail to Sand Dune Arch then cross the field to Broken Arch. Keep hiking to the end of the campground before returning to see the Tapestry Arch and sandstone fins.

If you have a little more time to spend in the park then there are three hikes you can complete. In total, these three hikes should take you about half a day:
1. Hike the Devils Garden trail to view the spire called Dark Angel. On you way back, take the primitive trail if you want to challenge yourself on

some steep slopes. Only do this if you can tolerate heights and if you've had prior experience and training.
2. Take the unpaved road to a remote area known as Klondike Bluffs and take the primitive hiking trail to the Tower Arch.

BRYCE CANYON, UTAH

If it is your first visit to Bryce Canyon and you only have a day, it may be a good idea to stick to the 18-mile scenic drive that offers 13 viewpoints over various amphitheaters. Although there are over 50 miles of trails to enjoy, at least eight of these trails can be hiked in less than a day.

For some quick and easy hikes consider Mossy Cave, Bristlecone Loop, and Queens Garden trails. All three of these are less than two miles. If you want something longer to do during the day then go for the Rim Trail that overlooks the entire amphitheater in 5.5 miles.

If you want to get into the wilderness on your day trip or just want to stay away from the crowds then consider the Fairyland Loop. This trail takes you down into the amphitheater and through several hoodoos, deep canyons, and natural bridges.

The highlight along this trail is the China Wall which features a row of ridge-top hoodoos that look like the Great Wall of China. Be aware that this hike is considered strenuous to do over 2,000 feet of elevation gain in eight miles.

For an entire day experience that is more unique than other hikes consider taking a horseback tour. There are several horseback tour options that take you back to the rugged old west days. Most of these tours are two to three hours-long and lead you down steep and narrow trails into the maze of the canyon.

These tours are often worthwhile, particularly for those who love horses

CANYONLANDS, UTAH

Canyonlands National Park is divided into five districts. It is nearly impossible to visit more than one district in a single day visit due to the massive extension of land they each cover. Thankfully, the majority of day hikes are found in Islands in the Sky and The Needles. Let's look at some of your day-trip itineraries in these districts.

You can visit both districts in a day if you embark on a driving tour of each. At Islands in the Sky you can drive to Grand View Point and get a grand view of the entire park. Along the way, stop at the Buck Canyon or Shafer Canyon Overlook if you have time.

In The Needles district you can take a two-hour drive of the three-mile unpaved Elephant Hill access road. If time permits, you can hike one or two of the short interpretive trails along the way.

If you have more time then you can pick one of the two districts and explore the scenery in a more thorough fashion on foot with some excellent hiking options.

Islands in the Sky District

After driving Grand View Point, you can stop at the Green River Overlook and hike the short half-mile loop to Mesa Arch and enjoy the nature trail. Other short nature trails you can enjoy as time permits during the day are the Whale Rock or Upheaval Dome.

The Needles District

Drive to Big Spring Canyon Overlook to enjoy breathtaking views. Get out and stretch your legs at a number of short trails as time allows. If you want to get a closer look at the district then consider the Slickrock Trail or Chesler Park. For a longer and more strenuous hike, take a backcountry trail.

CAPITOL REEF, UTAH

The best way to see Capitol Reef National Park if you only have a day is to choose one or more road tours through the park.

SCENIC DRIVE

This road trip starts at the Visitor Center and provides access to several roads including Grand Wash Road, Capitol Gorge Road, Pleasant Creek Road, and South Draw Road. This combined drive is 7.9 miles of paved road with dirt spur roads that can take you into the Grand Wash and the Capitol Gorge. This road trip isn't a loop, so you'll have to turn around and return on the same road.

SOUTH DRAW ROAD

This road is not maintained and will require a 4-wheel-drive. It takes you from Pleasant Creek to the park boundary near Tantalus Flats. In inclement weather this road is often impassable.

Notom-Bullfrog Road

This road connects to Utah Highway 24 about 9 miles east of the visitor center and extends south to the Glen Canyon National Recreation Area. The first 10 miles of this road is paved and then becomes a well-maintained dirt road. The road takes you along the east side of the Waterpocket Fold where you have plenty of hiking opportunities, as time allows.

Popular backcountry trails of Lower Muley Twist and Halls Creek Narrows can be accessed from this road. Check with the visitor center about the status of this road before attempting to drive it.

Burr Trail Road

This road follows an original cattle trail and goes from Boulder on Utah Highway 12 to the Notom-Bullfrog Road. The parts of this road in the national park take you past Circle Cliffs, Long Canyon, and The Gulch.

The road does feature many switchbacks that aren't appropriate for larger vehicles. Inside the park, the road is a graded dirt road and can be closed due to weather conditions, so check with the visitor center before traveling.

Hartnet Road

This road covers the southern half of the Cathedral Valley Loop and starts about 11 miles east of the visitor center off Utah Highway 24. In order to access this route to the Cathedral Valley you must ford the Fremont River so you'll need a high clearance vehicle. The conditions of this road will vary with the weather, so check before traveling.

Cathedral Road

This road includes the eastern side of the Cathedral Valley Loop and starts about 18 miles east of the visitor center. When you take this route into the Cathedral Valley you won't need to ford the Fremont River. Conditions will vary based on the weather, so check before traveling.

ZION, UTAH

Zion National Park offers a range of outdoor activities for travelers, but it is one of the easiest parks to navigate. At peak seasons– from early spring to late fall– you can take a free shuttle service from the nearby town of Springdale and throughout the park, so you can access all the trails without having to find a place for your vehicle.

Zion is an excellent destination to learn about canyoneering. This activity combines hiking, rappelling, problem solving, scrambling, and sometimes even swimming.

There are many canyons to explore here; some are for the casual explorer while others require a permit and more technical climbing skills.

The best place to start canyoneering is in The Narrows. This is the tightest part of Zion Canyon, at 2,000 feet high and only 20 to 30 feet wide in some areas. Along this hike you are able to enjoy views on one of the most impressive gorges by wading upstream through the Virgin River. You can access this hike just a mile from the shuttle stop.

If you are a more experienced hiker then you can try The Subway on the left fork of North Creek. You will need to get a permit for this hike and you can choose to explore the canyon from the bottom up– which requires scrambling and creek crossing for nine miles– or you can do it from the top down, which requires rappelling for 60 feet plus a little bit of swimming.

If you want to fully be a part of the signature Zion National Park hike, then take Angel's Landing. This hike perches you in the middle of the canyon 1,488 feet above the river.

However, this trail isn't easy and requires extensive climbing. Part of it is assisted by chains bolted into the rocks. So be prepared for a strenuous hike if you choose this one.

ROCKY MOUNTAIN, COLORADO

Most of the popular adventures at Rocky Mountain take place in the eastern portion of the park. The majority of your day hikes occur from two main trailheads: Glacier Gorge and Bear Lake. Both of these are popular for their access to alpine lakes.

Glacier Gorge Trail is a 9.6-mile out-and-back trail that takes you pass Mills Lake and Jewel Lake before reaching the end at Black Lake in a basin that sits above the treeline. Another popular trail off this is the Loch Trail / Sky Pond Trail, which is another 9 miles out and back to the Sky Pond surrounded by pine forests.

The Bear Lake Trailhead is one of the busiest in Rocky Mountain, and in the summer months the parking lot often fills up by 6:30am. Consider taking the free shuttle from the Beaver Meadows visitor center. This trail offers you a nice introduction the lakes of the area.

The Emerald Lake Trail takes you seven miles out-and-back, passing Nymph and Dream Lakes before ending at Emerald Lake. You can continue past Emerald Lake if you have time and hike to Tyndall Glacier, but this is a difficult and strenuous hike with about 1,800 feet of vertical scrambling.

There are also some simple and modest hiking options along Old Fall River Road. The most popular option is Chapin Pass Trailhead that guides you to a trio of mountain peaks: Mount Chapin, Mount Chiquita, and Ypsilon Mountain. These peaks are along an eight-mile mile trail on rolling, non-exposed class 2 hiking trail that is located all above the tree line.

For a longer and more challenging hike that could last for most of the day, consider Mount Ida. This 10-mile trail starts at Milner Pass Trailhead off Trail Ridge Road, and travels along the ridgeline that overlooks the Never Summer Mountains to the west. It is a non-technical trail that takes you from alpine meadows to a 12,880 foot summit along a smooth path. Along the way, you are likely to spot a variety of mammals such as elk, deer, and marmots.

The main artery in the park for visitors is Trail Ridge Road– a good place to explore if you only have a day to spend, as there is a lot to see. A local secret on the east side of the park is Wild Basin. In this region you can view waterfalls, lakes, and summits.

Some excellent trail options in the Wild Basin region are the 8.6-mile hike to Sand Beach Lake. The Wild Basin Trailhead also has numerous trails that are mostly flat. Some summits you can hike to in this area include Mount Alice, Tanima Peak, and Chiefs Head Peak.

For a more solitary experience, head to the western reaches of the park. From the East Inlet Trailhead you can hike to Spirit Lake and Lake Verna on a seven-mile round-trip adventure. If you start out at the Colorado River Trailhead, you will be able to choose a 6.2-mile round-trip trail to Lulu City, a ghost town with ruins to explore.

The North Inlet Trailhead is the perfect place for a 3.4-mile round-trip trail on Summerland Park to catch a glimpse of the largest wild mammal in Colorado, the moose. Be very careful, though, as moose are extremely temperamental and will get aggressive if they feel threatened.

MESA VERDE, COLORADO

The most popular activity for those visiting this park is the cliff dwellings. Three of the dwellings will require you to take a ranger guided tour: the Cliff Palace, the Balcony House, and Long House.

The largest cliff dwelling is Cliff Palace. While the total walking distance is 0.25 miles, there are approximately five, 8-10 foot ladders to climb in order to reach the dwelling.

The Balcony House is for a more adventurous hiker. You will need to climb a 32-foot ladder, crawl through a 12-foot tunnel, then climb two 10-foot ladders up a rock face in order to reach the dwellings. Not an easy hike, and definitely not recommended for those with claustrophobia, but otherwise it is well worth the effort.

Long House is the most in-depth ranger tour and features over 150 rooms on three levels. The hike is 2.25 miles and only involves two 15-foot ladders. Visitors are able to get up close to these dwellings and get a different view of life for Ancestral Puebloans.

Tours for all three of these dwellings are seasonal and are only offered during certain times of the year. If there isn't a tour available, you won't be able to see these dwellings.

The only dwelling that doesn't require you to take a ranger-led tour is the Step House on Wetherill Mesa. It allows you to explore at your own pace, but there is a ranger on-site to answer any questions you may have. You can explore the room and general layout as well as climbing down into an ancient kiva, which the Hopi used as a ceremonial room.

Second to the cliff dwellings is the act of looking for petroglyphs. The Petroglyph Point Loop isn't an easy hike, but it is the only trail that allows you to view petroglyphs up close.

The whole trail is a relatively short 2.4-mile round-trip with the petroglyph panel about 1.4 miles into the trail. Along the way you can enjoy beautiful views of the Spruce and Navajo Canyons below the mesa.

If you don't want to hike to the dwellings or don't have a lot of time, you can still drive around the park and see the dwellings from afar. This can also be a good option if you arrive in the off season when the dwellings are closed.

For wildlife-viewing, you best option is Prater Ridge Trail. The farther you get from the road, the more likely you are to see large mammals such as coyote or deer. The entire trail is 7.8 miles and leads you through woodland areas along the top of the ridge.

A lesser known choice is the trail on the Wetherill Mesa. This is a one-mile trail labeled Nordenskiold Site No. 16. While the journey is short, it will take you to an overlook of a cliff dwelling featuring 50 rooms with stone and sand-carved features.

GREAT SAND DUNES, COLORADO

There is plenty to see and do at the Great Sand Dunes National Park, as well as a wide range of ecosystems to explore and enjoy. However, if you only have a day to spend here and want to get the highlights, you will need to the main use area.

In two hours you can partake in six activities to give you a broad range of what the park has to offer. Start out in the visitor center to watch a film about the park and look at exhibits. Then you can head to the main dunefield from the main Dunes Parking Area. You can choose to hike or rent equipment to sand sled/board.

Seasonally, you can choose to get wet with a refreshing swim in Medano Creek after a hike or walk beneath the sun. If you have four-wheel-drive, go for a trip along Medano Pass Primitive Road to the Sand Pit or Castle Creek picnic area. If you have a dog, you can walk him or her along many of the picnic areas. Two excellent short hiking options are the Montville Nature Trail and Sand Sheet Loop Trail.

In three to five hours you can hike to the top of the first ridge of dunes. Make sure you do this early in the day to avoid the sun-heated sand in the afternoon. You can also take the time to head over toward the Zapata Falls Recreation Area to view a waterfall and a beautiful overview of the dunefield. Another option is to hike along Medano Creek and head into the mountains.

If you are going to spend the day in the park, consider attending an afternoon ranger program at the visitor center available on the weekends in the summer months. If you are there after dark, you could venture into the evening program at the Amphitheater. You can also hike the dunes at night to experience the natural sights, sounds, and clear starry skies reflecting upon cooling sand.

For excellent wildflower and bird-viewing opportunities, take a hike along Moca Pass. You can also hike the Star Dune, the tallest sand dune in North America. Around sunrise or sunset you can view elk, pronghorn, or mule deer in the grasslands.

BLACK CANYON OF THE GUNNISON, COLORADO

If you only have a day to spend at the Black Canyon, consider taking three scenic drives to give you a feel for the park. You'll surely want to return at a later date and spend several days exploring all the remaining qualities and memorable sights so characteristic of this location.

SOUTH RIM ROAD

This scenic drive is about seven miles long between Tomichi Point and High Point. Along the way, there are 12 overlooks for you to stop at and enjoy the breathtaking views. Most of the overlooks are reached by a short walking trail, so you have a chance to get out and stretch your legs.

Expect to take about two to three hours to reach several of the overlooks mentioned here. If you are limited on time, the main ones you want to stop at include: Gunnison Point, Chasm View, Painted Wall, and Sunset View. At Gunnison Point you can also step inside the visitor center to see some historical exhibits on the canyon. The visitor center is open daily in the summer.

North Rim Road

You access this road by taking a gravel road from the east end of Crawford State Park. Along the way, this road has six overlooks. Most of the canyon walls here are nearly vertical and offer impressive views not found anywhere else in the rest of the park. You should expect a leisurely drive to take you about two to three hours.

East Portal Road

The East Portal Road is a good option if you want to drive to the Gunnison River. The road also provides access to the Curecanti National Recreation Area where you can camp, picnic, and fish in clear waters surrounded by wildflowers and plenty of animals. This road is closed in the winter and isn't safe for the casual driver.

Expect steep grades of 16% or more and hairpin curves. Vehicles over 22 feet in length are prohibited on this road.

YELLOWSTONE, IDAHO/MONTANA/WYOMING

It is easy to see why people spend extended vacations at the first national park in the United States. If it is your first visit or you simply don't have a lot of time to spend, here are a few highlights of what you can do in a single day to get a taste of what the park is all about.

Any trip to Yellowstone must start at Gardiner, Montana, where you pass under the national park symbol: the Yellowstone Arch. This is an impressive entry point carved with Theodore Roosevelt's quote from 1903 that has become the national park creed, "For the Benefit and Enjoyment of the People". This is the point where the sightseeing begins.

Within just a couple minutes you'll arrive at Mammoth Hot Springs. This is the first of seven roadside thermal features within Yellowstone. You can choose to enjoy Mammoth from the road or you can walk the 1.75-mile boardwalk that gets you closer to the features.

Mammoth is a great way to introduce yourself to the power of geysers and the hot springs area, but remember you have a lot more to see and only a day to do it in during your stay at the park.

The next stop is the Norris Geyser Basin. Here you can hike 2.25 miles of trails and see the world's tallest active geyser. Norris is a beautiful place full of colorful hot springs.

As you continue south, you'll find Lower and Midway Geyser Basins. Midway provides you with magnificent views of Grand Prismatic Hot Springs and other geothermal features. Beyond this area is Upper Geyser Basin and the popular Old Faithful region.

Once you've finished touring the geysers and hot springs you can take the time to pick a place to hike. There are over 1,000 miles of trails that meet the hiking level of all visitors, so there are numerous varied trips suited to your personal preferences and abilities.

Some classic hikes you should consider exploring are Uncle Tom's Trail, the trails along the Grand Canyon of Yellowstone, and the Fountain Paint Pots Trail near Madison. You'll be able to enjoy an amazing panoramic view of Mount Washburn Trail at the top of Dunraven Pass after hiking upward toward the Elephant back, near the Fishing Bridge.

There is more to Yellowstone than just watching geysers and hiking the trails. You can also find absolutely lovely waterfalls very close to the main roads. If you have the opportunity to see only one, the most recommended option would be the Lower Falls located at the Grand Canyon of Yellowstone. Here you will enjoy some of the most iconic views in Yellowstone– Artist Point gives you the best views in this region.

Another excellent waterfall that can be seen after a short hike is Tower Falls, located a little more to the north. There is also Lewis Falls near the south entrance, in addition to Undine Falls east of Mammoth.

Something else you can do on a day trip is wildlife viewing. You can easily accomplish this activity at the many pull outs throughout the park. Bison and elk are often seen roaming valleys and forests, as most of the larger herds are located in the Lamar Valley in the northeastern part of the park. In this area you might also see wolves, bears, pronghorn, and nearly all mammals residing at Yellowstone, including the occasional moose.

Another place to view bison herds is at Hayden Valley, located in the middle of the park. Elk tend to stay near West Yellowstone and Mammoth where there are less predators, so that is the place to find them (with the necessary precautions).

While you'll want to spend the majority of your time exploring the outdoors, do make it a point to check out the history and beauty of the great lodges. Most of the lodges date back to the early days of the park and offer tours.

The Old Faithful Lodge is an example of a gorgeous architectural building that is just as iconic as the natural wonders of the park.

GRAND TETON, WYOMING

Whether it is your first time or you are a returning visitor, there are two excellent ways to experience Grand Teton in a day. The first is to go on a few scenic drives.

The second is to take the time to find a few designated viewing areas to observe both the wildlife and the natural beauty of their surroundings in a more relaxed fashion.

SCENIC DRIVES

There are a lot of turnouts along park roads that provide you with quick exhibits on park geology, wildlife, and plants. Turnouts are also a safe place to enjoy scenic views, wildlife, and photography opportunities. Consider the following scenic drives to behold all areas of the park.

The Teton Park Road is the main road that follows the base of the Teton Ridge and takes you from Moose to Jackson Lake Junction.

Another option is the Jenny Lake Scenic Drive guiding you along the east shore of Jenny Lake and offering you excellent views of the peaks. You can access this scenic drive from the North Jenny Lake Junction. Drive west towards the mountains, then turn left or south onto the one-way scenic drive. This scenic road joins the Teton Park Road just north of South Jenny Lake.

Lastly, Signal Mountain Summit Road takes you 800 feet up to panoramic landscapes of the Teton Range, Jackson Hole Valley, and Jackson Lake. Along the way, you'll find two overlooks that provide astounding observation points of the valley.

WILDLIFE VIEWING

If you get tired of driving the park, find a scenic spot to pull off and enjoy the scenery while watching the native wildlife. Let's look at some of the best places to view wildlife in Grand Teton National Park.

The first stop is Oxbow Bend about one mile east of Jackson Lake Junction. The slow moving waters here provide a unique habitat for fish like suckers and trout, which in turn attract river species such as otters, ospreys, bald eagles, white pelicans, and common mergansers. You may even see the occasional beaver or muskrat. The nearby willows that fill the river's edge often have moose and elk.

Another option is Timbered Island, a forested ridge located southwest of Jenny Lake. Here you'll be able to see small bands of pronghorn antelope, one of the fastest land animals in North America. At dawn and dusk you might catch a glance at a few elk as they eat the grasses growing in among the sagebrush.

One other destination is located east of US Highway 26/89/191 and about a mile north of Moose Junction. Along Mormon Row and Antelope Flats Road you'll find both bison and pronghorn grazing in the spring, summer, and fall months. Keep your eye out for coyotes, Northern harriers, and American kestrels, as they all hunt for small mammals and insects that frequent the area.

Yet another option is the Jackson Lake Dam just south of Moose. This is a grassy meadow near a river as well as a popular grazing area for elk and bison. You'll also be able to witness bald eagles, ospreys, and great blue herons flying toward their large stick nests. In the water and nearby areas you'll have a chance to see beavers and moose.

Just west of Jenny Lake is an area known as Inspiration Point. This is a common area to find gold-mantled ground squirrels. In addition, the boulder fields are a popular spot for the illusive pikas and marmots. At the mouth of the canyon there are shrubs where mule deer and moose like to browse.

The canyon is a popular nesting area for songbirds. Be aware that ground animals such as the squirrels will beg for food, but you shouldn't feed them human snacks or else it will hurt their digestive system. Instead, you could do a quick bit of research and pack foods such as nuts or seeds that are closer to what they regularly eat in their environment.

Lastly, some about a half-mile north of Moose along US Highway 26/89/191 at Blacktail Pond, you'll encounter old beaver ponds that have filled in with sediment and support grassy meadows that are popular grazing areas for elk in the cooler moments of the day.

You'll find numerous ducks in the side channels of the Snake River. Moose have also been known to browse along the river's edge.

GLACIER, MONTANA

Glacier National Park is a wonderful place for biking, hiking, and camping. The park is home to over 600 lakes so you can even come for a day of boating and fishing. The park service has the option of renting out canoes and kayaks. Consider boating from the Swiftcurrent Lake in the Many Glacier area to Lake Josephine if you want a quiet and peaceful day out on the water.

If you prefer to stay on land and want to see as much of the park in a day as possible then consider driving the Going-to-the-Sun Road. This 50-mile drive takes you through the center of the park and is listed as one of the most scenic roads in the United States. There are a few must stops along this road.

First, Logan Pass is a wonderful place to stop and stretch your legs. If time allows, take the 1.5-mile Hidden Lake hike. This is an easy and accessible trail. If you want a more peaceful hike away from crowds, consider the longer 7.6-mile Highline Trail.

However, be aware that this trail does require you to hike a sheer rock wall that has a cable hung along its side. If you can brave it you will not only be rewarded with excellent views as you parallel the Continental Divide, but also with an extreme surge of happiness at having defeated the obstacle in your way.

The heart of the park is the Many Glacier area, home to many popular hiking options that you can do within the day. The most well-visited hike is the one that takes you to Grinnell Glacier. It is an 11-mile round-trip hike that starts at the Many Glacier Hotel and takes you to Lake Josephine, then through meadows to a 1,600-foot climb up to the glacier viewpoint.

One trail that is often overlooked by most visitors is the Apikuni Falls Trail. It is just two miles and allows you to see a two-tiered cascading waterfall that is just stunning.

You won't be able to see the waterfall from the trailhead, but if you keep venturing forward, you will come face to face with the waterfall.

PART – 3

14-DAY PARK HOPPER TRAVEL PLANS

2-WEEK TRIP ITINERARIES

If you have two weeks to spare and want to take an in-depth trip at any of these national parks, there are some things you need to see.

I'm going to give you a couple sets of two-week trip itineraries so you have an idea of how you can spend a wonderful 14 days enjoying the beauty and outdoors at our National Parks.

ITINERARY #1: COLORADO

GREAT SAND DUNES, MESA VERDE, BLACK CANYON OF THE GUNNISON, ROCKY MOUNTAIN

These four parks are close enough together that you can choose to spend a few days at each, or you can pick one that is centrally located as a base and drive to each park from there.

You'll be able to spend at least three days exploring each park with a few extra days to catch the things you didn't think you had time for. Let's look at each park for some sightseeing ideas.

GREAT SAND DUNES

If you are going to stop at this national park for a few days, you must spend at least part of one day enjoying a unique activity that you can't do in any other park: sandboarding and sand-sledding.

These activities are allowed anywhere on the dunefield as long as it isn't near vegetated areas. From the main Dunes Parking Area it is at least a 0.7-mile hike to find small to medium-sized slopes, with the first high slope at about 1.25 miles away. Smaller slopes are great for those traveling with kids, while both adults and teens may have more fun on the taller slopes.

The National Park doesn't rent sleds or sandboards, but you can find them at three retailers in the San Luis Valley before heading into the park. Kristi Mountain Sports, 40 miles southwest of the Visitor Center have them available year-round as long as the sand isn't frozen.

Another option is Sand Dunes Swimming Pool and Recreation, 32 miles west of the Visitor Center near the town of Hooper. They are open every day all year except Thursdays. Lastly, the Oasis Store just outside the park entrance is available April through October.

While it may seem like other items can work, it is best to use specially designed sandboards and sand sleds when doing this activity. Snow equipment only works on very wet sand after rain or snow– the sand at this park is often dry. Cardboard and plastic materials don't slid on the sand and often drag.

So it is best to stick with sandboards and sand sleds that are made specifically for the activity; they have an extra slick base and a special wax that allow them to safely slide down sand under the majority of conditions.

If you plan to sandboard or sand sled, make sure you head out in the early morning or late evening hours, especially throughout the summer. During sunny weather, the surface of the sand can easily reach 150 degrees Fahrenheit or higher, and thunderstorms are possible.

Even if sand temperatures are mild during the spring and fall, the afternoons can tend to be pretty windy and the sand may get in your eyes or nose or mouth if you do not have the proper equipment.

If sliding down the dunes doesn't sound fun to you or if you prefer to go somewhere cooler during the heat of the day, consider hiking some of the forested trails and alpine trails. This is an excellent way to enjoy the other beautiful natural parts of the park without the heat.

FORESTED TRAILS

Your best option for avoiding the heat is the Montville Nature Trail. You will be able to marvel at and photograph Mt. Herard, the dunes, and the green valley at the highest point of the trail.

Another option is the Mosca Pass Trail, which follows a small creek to the summit of the lowest pass in the Sangre de Cristo Mountains. The trail takes you through aspen and evergreen forests. The hike goes on for about two to three hours in order to travel the three and a half miles. This same route was once used by the American Indians and early settlers to travel into the valley.

Lastly, if you want to explore the forests you should consider the Sand Ramp Trail. This 11-mile trail is often used to access backpacking sites along the foothills. It also stays at the same elevation along the mountain base. The trail starts in Loop 2 of the campground or at the Point of No Return Parking Area. This can be a strenuous hike and you should allow a pocket of extra time to hike the trail.

Hiking the alpine trails is also a great way to venture further into the forest.

Alpine Trails

Your first route is the Medano Lake and Mount Herard hike. The trailhead is accessed from the Medano Pass 4WD Road. It starts at a 10,000 feet elevation and climbs 2,000 feet through meadows and forests before ending at the timberline and a beautiful alpine lake. More advanced hikers can choose to continue on to the summit of Mount Herard at 13,297 feet. At this summit, you will encounter unparalleled landscape sights of the dunes below.

For a longer hike and/or drive you can head to Music Pass, Sand Creek Lakes, and other alpine peaks. From November to June, check conditions before heading out since snow may block some of the trails or possibly endanger you with flash floods during the thunderstorm season.

The Music Pass trailhead is accessed east of Highway 69 about 4.5 miles south of Westcliffe. Turn off Highway 69 to the west at the sign for Music Pass. At the T junction, turn left onto South Colony Road. At the end of the ranch fence you'll see a sign on your right for the Music Pass Trailhead. 2WD vehicles should park at the point where Rainbow Trail crosses Music Pass Road, then walk 3.5 miles to the pass.

Those with 4WD vehicles can drive another 2.5 miles to the end of the road and just take a steep one-mile hike to the pass. The pass is located at the tree line facing the Upper Sand Creek basin. After reaching the pass you can continue to hike to four alpine lakes or to any of the peaks above the basin at 13,000 feet. From Music Pass Summit you have three options:

1. Lower Sand Creek Lake: 3 miles
2. Upper Sand Creek Lake: 3.5 miles
3. Little Sand Creek Lakes: 8 miles

MESA VERDE

People primarily come to Mesa Verde National Park to see the cliff dwellings of ancient civilizations. You can visit these historic and cultural sites through guided tours and self-guided tours. However, this isn't the main focus of the park– there are also a many natural landmarks and picturesque sights to explore in other hikes.

Let's take a look at your many options available for when you have several days to stay at this park.

GUIDED TOURS

Ranger-guided tours take you to Cliff Palace, Balcony House, and Long House, all of which are very popular. You can often tour at least two of these areas in a single day with prior planning. Be aware that the tours are strenuous and you should be in good physical condition and equipped with plenty of water before undertaking them.

The tours have no height or age restrictions, but children need to be able to hike trails, climb ladders, and navigate steps on their own. Infants can be carried in a backpack if the adult can maintain mobility and balance. Tour tickets must be purchased in person at the park.

Cliff Palace is the largest cliff dwelling in the park. The ranger-guided tour of this site is one-hour long and requires climbing five 8-10 foot ladders on a 100-foot vertical climb. The total walking distance is only about ¼ mile round-trip. The tour starts at Cliff Palace Overlook and is a 23-mile, or one-hour, drive from the visitor center. For a unique experience you can also take a Cliff Palace Twilight Tour.

For the more adventurous type of folks: you can try the Balcony House tour. This one-hour tour includes climbing a 32-foot ladder, crawling through a 12-foot tunnel and climbing a 60-foot open rock face with two 10-foot ladders in order to exit the site. The tour starts in the Balcony House parking lot and is about a 25-mile or about an hour-long drive from the visitor center.

Lastly, the Long House tour is the longest ranger-guided tour in the park. It starts at the Wetherill Mesa information desk and takes two hours to complete. Throughout the tour you will hike at least 2.25 miles' worth of a round-trip as well as climb two 15-foot ladders within the cliff dwelling site.

The hike does have an elevation gain of about 130 feet, and ends at the Long House Trailhead. You can either return to the kiosk or continue exploring the rest of Wetherill Mesa on your own. Allow about an extra cushion of time to return to the kiosk after the two-hour tour.

If you're traveling to the park in mid-April to mid-October, you also have the option of taking a half-day guided bus tour. Aramark Leisure, the concessionaire for Mesa Verde National Park, offers bus tours with modern views of the ancient cliff dwellings. The tours cover 700 years of history. You can purchase tickets for these tours at the Mesa Verde Visitor Center, Far View Lodge and Terrace, and Morefield Campground.

If you would prefer to explore on your own then you have several options.

Self-Guided Tours

There are still plenty of cultural sites in the park to explore on your own. Some of these sites are open year-round while others are open seasonally, so take a look at the park schedule when planning your trip. Let's start by looking at some of these cultural sites you can visit on your own and at your own pace.

From early March to early November you can stop at the best preserved cliff dwelling at Spruce Tree House. There are viewpoints near the Chapin Mesa Archeological Museum and rangers are there daily from 9am to 4pm to share information or answer any questions you may have.

Alternatively, you could take an auto tour along Mesa Top Loop Road that covers 700 years of Mesa Verde history as well. This six-mile driving tour has several short paved trails you can take along the way for a wonderful day trip. Along this path, you can also stop to explore 12 easily-accessible sites that range from surface dwellings to cliff dwelling overlooks.

Some must-see stops include Square Tower House, Sun Point Overlook, and panoramic landscapes of Cliff Palace from Sun Point and Sun Temple.

You can also visit the Far View Sites Complex, a grouping of five mesa top villages and the far view reservoir. These are located on a level ¾-mile unpaved trail, four miles north of the Chapin Mesa Archeological Museum. It is open from 8am to sunset.

Cedar Tree Tower is a mesa top tower and kiva that you can view from the road and is also open from 8am to sunset.

The Step House is a pithouse, petroglyphs location, and cliff dwelling. It takes a winding path that involves 100 feet of descent and ascent. The total walking distance is about a mile round-trip and will take you about 45 minutes to an hour. The trail starts at the Wetherill Mesa Kiosk.

Lastly, the Badger House Trail guides you to four mesa top sites. This 2.25-mile round-trip trail takes you through the Badger House Community that starts at the Wetherill Mesa Kiosk. This walk will take you through 600 years of prehistoric times. The trail is a combination of gravel and pavement, and it is open from early May to late October.

Once you've had your fill of historical and cultural sites, consider going on some nature hiking trails to enjoy the natural beauty of the park.

Hiking Trails

First up is the Prater Ridge Trail at a 7.8-mile round-trip. This trail starts at the west end of Morefield Campground, climbs up Prater Ridge, and follows a loop around the top before returning by the same route. There is a cut-off trail you can take that shortens the trail to only five miles.

There is also the Knife Edge Trail that is a short two-mile round-trip. The trail follows a section of the old Knife Edge Road at the northwest corner of Morefield Campground near the Montezuma Valley Overlook. While hiking this trail you'll be able to bask in gorgeous sights of the Montezuma Valley. The old road is actually the original main access to the park in 1914.

Point Lookout Trail is another simple 2.2-mile round-trip trail. It switchbacks up Point Lookout and travels across the top of the mesa. The trail gives you an opportunity to glimpse at both Montezuma and Mancos Valleys and the nearby countryside.

To see nature and history at the same time, consider Petroglyph Point Trail at a 2.4-miles round-trip. This trail is for the adventurous hiker and gives you with open scenes of both Spruce and Navajo Canyons. Along the way, about 1.4 miles from the trailhead, you can explore a large petroglyph panel.
The trail is narrow and rugged with several step drop-offs along the canyon wall. There is also a large stone staircase that requires the use of hands and feet to climb to the top. However, the return is an easy forest loop. This trailhead is near the Chapin Mesa Archeological Museum. To hike this route, you will need to register at the trailhead or the museum.

Explore the canyons of the park with the Spruce Canyon Trail at a 2.4-mile round-trip. This trail follows the bottom of Spruce Tree Canyon and returns through the museum and picnic area. The trailhead starts at the Chapin Mesa Archeological Museum. You will need to register beforehand, but it ought to be a quick task. You'll be enveloped in a storm of colors and scents found in wildflowers at their full bloom, and marvel at a few talkative squirrels or birds all throughout the journey.

For a simple trail that allows you to look at the canyons from the top consider the Soda Canyon Overlook Trail. This 1.2-mile round-trip hike begins north of Balcony House in the parking area with Cliff Palace Loop Road.

The trail guides you through a simple walk to the canyon edge and provides you with an unparalleled archaeological experience along the canyon.

Another option for exploring history and nature at the same time is the Farming Terrace Trail. At only a half-mile round-trip, this hike takes you to a series of prehistoric check dams that were built by the ancestral Puebloans to create farming terraces. You'll also see a lot of native plants along this trail.

Another good historic trail is Nordenskiold Site No. 16. This two-mile round-trip trail starts at the information kiosk and is a leisurely and quiet hike. Due to a fire in 2000, there is no shade on this trail, so come prepared with proper sun-protecting equipment.

Black Canyon of the Gunnison

At Black Canyon of the Gunnison National Park the main choice of activity is hiking. In fact, the majority of hikes at this park are strenuous and require an experienced hiker.

Many trails have steep drop-offs and are not recommended for children or those who aren't steady on their feet. There are several hikes to explore throughout the park that don't take you down into the canyon.

South Rim

Rim Rock Nature Trail is a one-mile round-trip moderate hike. This is a self-guided nature trail that follows a flat path following the canyon rim. This sunny route features a wide variety of plant life. There are also several places along the trail that allow you to view the Gunnison River and the sheer rock walls of the canyon. The trailhead is located near the entrance to Campground Loop C and ends at the Visitor Center for the South Rim.

Another option is the Oak Flat Loop Trail. This two-mile round-trip hike is strenuous. This unique trail allows hikers to explore below the rim without actually having to hike to the river.

Be aware that this trail is narrow in places and requires climbing some steep slopes. The trail starts at the visitor center.

An easier alternative route is the Cedar Point Nature Trail at a short ⅔-mile trip. Needless to say, the trail is short, sunny, and has a moderate slope. Along the way there are guideposts that describe local flora seen throughout the hike.

At the end of the trail you can enjoy two overlooks of the river some 2,000 feet below. You'll also be able to view the famous Painted Wall, the tallest cliff in Colorado standing at over 2,000 feet.

A moderate level is Warner Point Nature Trail at a 1.5 miles round-trip. There is a trail guide that you can get at the High Point Overlook or the South Rim Visitor Center. The trail offers several shaded benches where you can rest and take in the scenery.

North Rim

The Chasm View Nature Trail is a short ⅓-mile round-trip moderate hike. It is accessed from the end of the one-way campground loop. After hiking through the forest, you come to the North Chasm View at about 1,800 feet above the river. The trail continues along the rim until you get to a second overlook of the Painted Wall and Serpent Point.

Another option is the North Vista Trail that can be divided into two separate hikes depending on your hiking level and time you have. Hiking to Exclamation Point is a moderate, three-mile long round-trip. The second out of the two consists of a hike to Green Mountain, which is a strenuous seven-mile round-trip.
However, this trail allows you to enjoy some of the best scenic views in the park. It trail starts at the North Rim Ranger Station. At Exclamation Point you can relax while viewing the complex waves and patterns of the inner canyon. If you continue to the Green Mountain, you will enjoy panoramic views of San Juan Mountains, the West Elks, Grand Mesa, the Uncompahgre Plateau, and the Black Canyon.

For an easy to moderate hike, consider the five-mile long Deadhorse Trail. The trail allows you to view Deadhorse Gulch and the East Portal of the Gunnison River. It is also an excellent trail for those interested in birding, and was actually an old service road that started at the old Ranger Station near the Kneeling Camel Overlook.

If you are a more adventurous outdoor individual who wants a challenge, go for a satisfying hike at the inner canyon. This can be a good option if you want to spend several days at the park.

INNER CANYON HIKING

The inner canyon has no maintained or marked trails. The routes are difficult to follow and you should only attempt these hikes if you are in good physical shape and had previous training.

You will be expected to find your own way and prepare to rescue yourself if needed. This requires owning a map and all the needed equipment for the occasion.

ROUTES ALONG THE NORTH RIM

Those who are new to the North Rim inner canyon should consider the S.O.B. Draw. This trail is known for poison ivy, so it is recommended you wear long pants. You can park in the pull through near the campground registration board or at the North Rim Ranger Station. The route starts at the access ladder along the fence line at the east end of the campground.

There are short ledges of climb, and the campsites are located downstream. This route is about 1.75 miles with a vertical drop of 1,800 feet, and a descent typically takes two hours with the ascent taking three hours. River access is two miles away. There are six campsites.

Another option is Long Draw, formally known as Devil's Slide. This path takes you to some of the narrowest parts of the canyon along the Gunnison River. You can park at the Balanced Rock Overlook and then head northeast. There are short ledges to climb as well as lots of poison ivy at the bottom of the route, so proceed with the utmost discretion.

This path is one mile long with river access at the first quarter mile with a vertical drop of 1,800 feet. It might be a slippery slope at times, but it is well-worth it once you get to see your surroundings. There is one campsite which may get crowded during the peak seasons. The descent takes 1.5 hours and the ascent another three hours– it is, overall, a one-day trip at the very least.

The next trip in the list is Slide Draw. This route is very steep and can be dangerous due to loose rocks and difficult footing. Only the more experienced type of hiker ought to opt for this route. There is a 30-foot climb downward to start the path. You can park at Kneeling Camel View and then head east until you reach the draw.

The draw takes you to the river where you'll find a good camping area. The path is one mile long with river access at three quarters of the first mile and a vertical drop of 1,620 feet. There are two campsites that offer plenty of room for the wary hiker. A descent takes one hour and a half, while the ascent takes four hours.

ROUTES ALONG THE SOUTH RIM

The most popular route to the inner canyon is the Gunnison Route, but it is still a very strenuous path. It is another alternative for those who are taking their first inner canyon hike and are in the mood for a challenge of sorts. A third of the way down you'll find an 80-foot chain.

The path starts at the South Rim Visitor Center. An outhouse and campsites are located upstream at the pitstop. The path is one mile long with river access at three quarters of the first mile with a vertical drop of 1,800 feet. There are three campsites. A descent takes 1.5 hours and an ascent two hours.

A more challenging part of the list involves the Tomichi Route and it is considered one of the steepest and most difficult paths on the south rim. The entire trail is full of loose rocks and a whole lot of sun exposure. You can park at the South Rim Campground to access this trail.

The trail is one mile long with river access at the half-mile mark and a vertical drop of 1,960 feet. There are two campsites. A descent takes 1.5 hours and an ascent takes 4.5 hours, or triple your descent time.

The Warner Route is the longest option and it is recommended you pack and plan for an overnight trip. There are campsites both upstream and downstream.

Hike the Warner Point Nature Trail until you see a small silver sign stating "Serviceberry Bush" which is the start of the Warner Route. The path is 2.75 miles with river access after the first mile and a vertical drop of 2,722 feet. There are five campsites. Descent takes two to 2.5 hours and the ascent takes four hours.

ROUTES ALONG THE EAST PORTAL

There are two main possibilities in this section of the park. Your first option is Devil's Backbone Route. Hike down the south side for about a half mile until you reach a ridge that runs down the cliff. The downstream side is easier, as it has small ridgelines to hike over along the way.

A second option is the North River Route. At the registration board you can find a good landing to boat across the river for this route. Once you cross the river, you can hike about two miles down from the river to the cliff at Flat Rock Rapid. You only have one low ridge to hike over at Deadhorse Gulch.

ROCKY MOUNTAIN

Rocky Mountain National Park is a excellent place to spend three or more days and enjoy a range of hiking spots. There are over 355 miles of hiking trails of all shapes and sizes– everything from flat lakeside trails to steep mountain peaks.

If you are new to the park you can talk with rangers at the visitor centers or backcountry offices to determine the best trails for your fitness and previous experience.

As you think about which hikes you want to take, keep in mind that the park's elevation varies radically from 7,500 to over 12,000 feet. Even at lower elevations a fit individual may experience altitude sickness. Some symptoms to look for include headaches, shortness of breath, insomnia, and rapid heartbeat. It often takes a few days for your body to adapt to higher elevations, but full acclimation can take weeks.

To avoid these symptoms make sure you drink plenty of water, avoid alcohol, eat all your meals, and get as much rest as possible. While you may not feel thirsty, the thinner the air gets at higher altitudes actually increases water evaporation from your lungs. So, to reiterate: staying hydrated will prevent some of the symptoms.

Also, when hiking in the mountains, be aware that ultraviolet light is stronger since it is a higher altitude and the sunlight will hit you in a more direct fashion than if there were clouds or branches and other layers between you and the sun. This means you should wear sunscreen, a hat, sunglasses, and a long-sleeved shirt if you are going to be walking or hiking for long periods of time.

Now let's consider some more recommended hikes to take while you're staying in the park.

LAKE HIKE CHART

Lake	Trail	Distance	Elevation Gain
Bear Lake	Bear Lake Trail	0.6-mile loop	Mild
Cub Lake	Cub Lake Trail	2.3 miles	540 feet
Mills Lake	Glacier Gorge Trail	2.8 miles	700 feet
Bluebird Lake	Wild Basin Trail	6 miles	2,478 feet

WATERFALL HIKE CHART

Waterfall	Trail	Distance	Elevation Gain
Adams Falls	East Inlet Trail	0.3 miles	Mild
Alberta Falls	Glacier Gorge Trail	0.6 miles	210 feet
Cascade Falls	North Inlet Trail	3.5 miles	300 feet
Ouzel Falls	Wild Basin Trail	2.7 miles	960 feet
Timberline Falls	Glacier Gorge Trail	4 miles	1,510 feet

SUMMIT HIKE CHART

Mountain	Trail	Distance	Elevation Gain
Deer Mountain	Deer Ridge Trail	3 miles	1,093 feet
Twin Sisters Peaks	Twin Sisters Trail	3.7 miles	2,253 feet
Flattop Mountain	Bear Lake Trail	4.4 miles	2,849 feet

ITINERARY #2: UTAH

ARCHES, CANYONLANDS, CAPITOL REEF, BRYCE CANYON, ZION

Another excellent two-week vacation itinerary is to visit most of the national park found in Utah. You can plan your trip by staying in a central park and traveling to the rest or you can spend two to three days at a park before driving to the next one. It all depends on how much you plan to do during that time.

Let's take a look at some more in-depth activities that are typical in each of these regions.

ARCHES

When staying in Arches for a few days consider visiting one or two areas of the park. Because there are a lot of things to see and do, you'll still be limited if you only spend a couple days at this location. It is time to check out all the various surrounding areas and their designated activities so you have a better idea of how much you wish to see throughout your stay.

PARK AVENUE AND COURTHOUSE TOWERS

Once you pass the visitor center you can climb steep switchback roads to reach the main area of the park. Here you can walk among monoliths and walls with views of the La Sal Mountains in the background.

Beyond the Park Avenue Viewpoint you can continue on a hiking trail that steeply descends into the canyon and continues one mile toward the Courthouse Towers. Retrace your steps along the trail for a round-trip hike.

You should also check out the La Sal Mountains Viewpoint where you can get a 360 degree view from a sandstone beach. To the east you can see the La Sal Mountains and other distinctive formations such as the Three Gossips, Sheep Rock, and the Organ all located within the Courthouse Towers area.

BALANCED ROCK

This destination features one of the most iconic features of the park: a staggering 128-foot tall formation. It isn't really a balanced rock; the Entrada Sandstone is a slick boulder that is attached to the eroding Dewey Bridge mudstone underneath. Eventually, this formation will disappear so you certainly want to take the time to view it now.

Unlike other features in the park, you can see this one from the park road. It is about 9.2 miles from the visitor center. While parking is limited, you can hike a short distance of about 0.3 miles; worth of a round-trip to observe the Balanced Rock up close. This is also a great place to go at night after a day in the park to stargaze and do some night photography.

The stars look particularly beautiful, away from all sorts of light pollution. You could even plan for a trip that falls around a scheduled meteor shower and bring a couple of telescopes and a few blankets to experience a sight you will never forget.

Across from Balanced Rock is a wonderful picnic area along a gravel road. Here you can enjoy a meal with the Salt Valley and Balanced Rock in the background.

THE WINDOWS SECTION

This is often considered the heart of the national park. You'll see a large group of scenic arches. A few of the better-known sites in the area are North Window,

Turret Arch, and Double Arch. Other features a little farther apart include Garden of Eden, Elephant Butte, and Parade of Elephants.

The Windows Section is nine miles north on the park road and 2.5 miles east on the Windows road. Drive time from the visitor center is about 25 minutes. The Windows Section is a great option if you are low on time and don't want a strenuous hike.

Take a gentle climb up a gravel trail to the North Window, South Window, and Turret Arch– about a 0.7-mile round-trip. You can return to the parking lot by the same trail or take a slightly longer and more primitive trail around the Windows starting at the South Window viewpoint, making for a one-mile round-trip trail.

The Double Arch Trail is a half-mile round-trip trail on a flat, gravel-surfaced path that takes you to the base of two huge arches. Double Arch is the tallest standing at 112 feet, and the second tallest at 144 feet. You can also view this arch from the parking lot if you don't want to hike.

While the Windows parking lot is large, it often fills to capacity. You may want to go to another area and come back at a different time to avoid congestion and heat. It is best to go in the early morning or late afternoon hours.

DELICATE ARCH

Visiting this arch is one of the things on most people's to-do list– in fact, it has become the symbol of the state of Utah and is even one of the most famous geologic features in the world. At 46 feet tall and 32 feet wide it is the largest free-standing arch in the park. It is difficult to see it from the main road and you'll need to get out of your vehicle to actually appreciate it.

You can walk 100 yards to the Lower Delicate Arch Viewpoint where you can see the arch from a mile away. Another half-mile walk takes you to the Upper Viewpoint with a less obstructed view, but it does require going up some stairs.

The trail to catch a close-up glimpse of the arch is a three-mile round-trip that climbs upward to 480 feet. It is a steady uphill trail that also takes you past Wolfe Ranch cabin and a wall of petroglyphs from the Ute Indians. Before taking this hike consider your health and fitness, as it is hot in the summer and often icy and dangerous in the winter.

On busy days, the parking lot at Wolfe Ranch Trailhead fills with large crowds. There is additional parking at the Delicate Arch Viewpoint parking lot. If you park at the viewpoint, you will need to hike an additional mile along the road to reach the trailhead.

The total round-trip hike will be five miles. This trail is often busy throughout the year, particularly during sunsets, where hundreds of people gather to take photographs or to have picnics.

Devil's Garden

This is a great spot to head for adventure. You can hike among arches, spires, and numerous thin rock walls known as "fins". The main landscape feature is the Landscape Arch, the longest arch in the United States, standing at 306 feet.

The arch is only six feet in diameter at its narrowest, interestingly enough. Other similar arches have fallen in recent years, so it is only a matter of time before this arch disappears forever as well.

This section located at the end of the park road, about 18 miles north of the visitor center; the drive will take you approximately 45 minutes. There is a campground nearby that is open from March through October with reservation, and during the winter months it is first come, first served.

Devil's Garden Trail is 1.6 miles and leads you to the Landscape Arch on a relatively flat trail. There is no elevation gain, just moderate hills that gently go up and down. There are two easy spurs you can choose to take to Pine Tree Arch and Tunnel Arch. Beyond the Landscape Arch, the hike becomes more difficult and leads to Double O Arch. If you want to avoid a challenging hike, you should turn around at this point.

The trail that guides you to Double O Arch is difficult, since it steeply climbs upward and on top of sandstone fins. The footing is rocky, as it has narrow ledges with drop-offs. There are some areas where hikers will have to use their hands and feet to scramble. Although strenuous, the hike is 4.2-mile round-trip and has gained a reputation and popularity amongst hikers.

Along the way there is the option of take two short spur trails to Navajo Arch and Partition Arch. These are located about one third of the way between Landscape and Double O Arch.

There is a quick spur trail to Dark Angel after a 0.8-mile round-trip. It begins on the north side of Double O Arch and walks you to the tall, dark spire that you see in the distance from Double O Arch.

Another option to get to or from Double O Arch is the Primitive Trail. It is 2.2 miles one-way and is the most difficult part of the Devils Garden trail system. Some of the obstacles you'll find here are steep slopes, narrow drop offs, and rock scrambling. You will also be required to cross a pool that may contain water at certain times of the year.

A spur trail takes you into a 0.1-mile round-trip to the Primitive Arch. Both of these trails are not recommended when the rock is wet or icy, which would be during the winter and spring seasons. It is also not recommended for individuals who have trouble with heights.

CANYONLANDS

Canyonlands National Park is divided into five districts with the majority of activities taking place in Islands in the Sky and the Needles districts. You'll need at least two full days to explore both of these sections, but stay a few extra days if you want to explore all the areas of the park.

For those short on time, take the popular Mesa Arch Trail. It is a short half-mile round-trip that ends at Mesa Arch, which frames Buck Canyon below and the La Sal Mountains in the distance. It is best to take this hike in the early morning hours or at sunset.

If you want a bit more of a challenge, you should consider the steep Gooseberry Canyon Trail. This 5.4-mile round-trip hike drops about 1,000 feet in just a mile before turning into a gentler slope. Gooseberry Canyon is full of switchbacks with intense sunlight exposure. However, the sights you'll find of the canyon are well worth the effort.

Islands in the Sky District has a 5.8-mile Neck Spring Loop trail that passes by the remains of historic ranching activity, two springs, and various native plant species. It is a moderate hike with just 300 feet of elevation change.

If you like to mountain bike you should head over toward the Lathrop Canyon Trail. It is an eight-mile round-trip hike taking off from White Rim Trail and leading you to the Colorado River. You'll see a vast array of plant life throughout this road.

Islands in the Sky Mesa is a popular destination for climbers due to its sandstone towers. The district is located in the northernmost tip of the park and is accessed through the White Rim Trail. Climbing in other portions of the park is difficult since there is poor rock quality and no pre-established routes. There are actually several sections of the park where climbing is prohibited in order to ensure the safety of all visitors.

Perhaps one of the most important activities in Canyonlands is spending the night and enjoying stargazing at the night sky. Canyonlands is one of the best places to see the stars at night since there is absolutely no light pollution and no towering buildings blocking your eyes from the firmament. Throughout the summer there are organized stargazing events that you can take part in during your overnight stay.

In the Needles District there is the 11-mile Chesler Park Loop that is great for viewing spires and buttes in the park. There are also six primitive campgrounds if you want to backpack and return to a safe location in order to rest. Chesler Park is a broad valley that you can hike through while admiring the surrounding rock formations and massive boulders.

Another option is the Lower Red Lake Canyon route at a 19-mile round-trip that takes you from Elephant Hill to the Colorado River. There are 1,400 feet of elevation gain and very little shade, so it is a more complicated multi-day hike.

A lesser known, quieter trail is the Sims-Hesse-Hanning Route in the Islands in the Sky District. It is a 5.11-mile route that offers views of the Green River below with several areas for technical climbing.

The 100-mile White Rim Road Trail is definitely recommended for mountain bikers. It can also be done as a backpacking trip, but would easily take three to five days to complete. There are campgrounds along this route, but they are remote, offer no services, and require a permit. No matter which way you choose to do this trail, expect to get a steep climb at the end of your hike.

While Islands in the Sky and the Needles are the two most common districts people explore, so you can head to The Maze District if you want more peace and quiet. This remote destination will require a four-wheel drive, a good topographical map, and a GPS device (as well as knowledge on how to use all of this equipment, just to be clear).

Consider the Harvest Scene Route that takes you to a 3,700 year-old wall of painted rock art called the Harvest Scene Pictographs. It is a difficult 8.7-mile loop hike that starts at the Chimney Rock Trailhead and passes through two canyons. There are a few steep descents and ascents along the way, but you are rewarded with views of the massive Chocolate Drops on the canyon rim.

Lastly, you can see the park in a unique way by using boat across the Cataract Canyon. This portion of the Colorado River starts where the Green and Colorado Rivers meet and features two very difficult whitewater rapids along with calm flat waters afterward.

The best time to travel by boat in Canyonlands is the late summer and fall, when the water is low and you can stay on sandbars at night if needed.

CAPITOL REEF

There are dozens sightseeing and exploration options within the districts of Capitol Reef National Park, so we will mention as many as we can.

The Fruita Area is the most accessible district and offers several views along the paved Scenic Drive. There are a number of hikes offering varying lengths and difficulties as well as access to the Fruita Historic District including the orchards and the Gifford House Store and Museum.

When exploring the Fruita Area, start at the visitor center. Here you can view the park movie, exhibits, and information on the places you will see. Next, head to the historic Gifford House Store and Museum, open from spring to fall. Exhibits here showcase Mormon pioneer history as well as local handmade goods for sale.

You'll also want to take the time to visit the orchards. Capitol Reef maintains one of the largest historical orchards in the National Park Service, with over 3,000 trees of the apple, peach, pear, apricot, cherry, and plum varieties.

Flowering occurs from February into May, and harvest is from June to October. Whilst in the orchards, you are free to sample the sweet fruit, and you are only charged a small fee to remove said fruit from the orchard.

Three Types of Hiking Trails (Easy, Moderate & Strenuous)

Take the time to explore as many of the following trails you are interested in hiking.

Easy Hikes

- ☐ Goosenecks, 0.1 miles one-way – Magnificent canyon sights.
- ☐ Sunset Point, 0.4 miles one-way – Panorama best viewed at sunset.
- ☐ Capitol Gorge, 1 mile one-way – Deep canyon with historic inscriptions.
- ☐ Grand Wash, 2.2 miles one-way – Deep canyon with narrow passages.

MODERATE HIKES

- ☐ Cohab Canyon, 1.7 miles one-way – Hidden canyons, views of the area and panoramic viewpoints.
- ☐ Fremont River, 1 mile one-way – Follows the river then climbs to a viewpoint.
- ☐ Hickman Bridge, 0.9 miles one-way – Natural bridge and canyon panoramas.

STRENUOUS HIKES

- ☐ Cassidy Arch, 1.7 miles one-way – Natural arch and canyon vistas.
- ☐ Chimney Rock Loop, 3.6 miles round-trip – Panorama best viewed at sunset.
- ☐ Fremont Gorge Overlook, 2.3 miles one-way – Open mesa top and sights of rim.
- ☐ Frying Pan, 2.9 miles one-way – Ridgetop panoramas.
- ☐ Golden Throne, 2 miles one-way – Views of Capitol Gorge and Golden Throne.
- ☐ Old Wagon Trail, Loop 3.8 miles round-trip – Forest hike with outlooking the cliffs
- ☐ Rim Overlook, 2.3 miles one-way – Panoramas from a dramatic cliff edge.
- ☐ Navajo Knobs, 4.7 miles one-way – 360-degree mountain panorama.

A lesser-visited section of the park is the Waterpocket District which offers some hiking and plenty of backpacking options. The roads are unpaved and sometimes can only be accessed by 4WD. Check weather and road conditions before heading to this district.

The last destination here is Cathedral Valley, which is the best location for a backcountry experience. You'll often need a high-clearance vehicle to get to most of the features available. Again, check weather and road conditions before heading to this district.

Bryce Canyon

There is plenty to do in Bryce Canyon National Park. If you are going to be there a few days, you can get the most out of your visit by taking part in one or more guided Ranger Programs.

Beginning late spring through October, the Ranger Programs are scheduled every two weeks and you can get a current list of the events at the visitor center. Let's consider what some of your options may be.

Geology Talks

These lectures are available daily year-round and they often last a half hour. They take place at Sunset Point during spring, summer, and fall, and are switched to the Visitor Center Auditorium in the winter months. Many parts of Bryce Canyon have been studied by geologists, especially the ancient lake and frost-wedging, so the content is very informative.

Geology talks often cover the current scientific explanations about the unique history of this park. No reservations are needed to attend any of the presentations.

Rim Walk

This Ranger Program is offered daily in the spring, summer, and fall and occurs at Sunset Point. It is an hour and a half for a one-mile round=trip hike which offers breathtaking sights, native plants, and wildlife stories along with a little bit of geology and cultural history.

You'll not only get to learn about the park, but you'll also be able to hike along the rim of the Bryce Amphitheater. There are no reservations needed to partake in this activity.

KIDS PROGRAMS

These are offered almost daily in the summer and can be found at the North Campground Picnic Area, where they typically last an hour. While all Ranger Programs are family friendly, these are specifically geared towards both children and their parents.

Rangers present a wide range of topics on a variety of interests. The visitor center will have a list of program topics and age requirements. Sign up is done at the visitor center and children need to be accompanied by an adult.

EVENING PROGRAMS

Offered nightly in the summer and fall. The location varies, but they are typically one-hour long. These evening programs offer an in-depth way to learn interesting stories and compelling resources about the Bryce Canyon area. The visitor center will have a list of topics, start times, and locations.

FULL MOON HIKES

Occurs on full moon nights. Lotteries are held at the visitor center and Bryce Lodge which open at 4pm. The hikes last between two to three hours and can be one to two miles. This is a wonderful nocturnal adventure for those staying overnight in the park. Flashlights are prohibited on the hike.

ASTRONOMY PROGRAMS

Schedule varies as does location. The visitor center has specific information on this matter. The program is one hour and comes equipped with a multimedia show and stargazing with telescopes. Constellations, meteor showers, shooting stars, various phases of the moon, and even planets are all visible and explored.

The night sky in Bryce Canyon is very beautiful and it is a great experience to enjoy if you are staying overnight in the park.

SNOWSHOE HIKES

Available in the winter when snow depth and staffing allows. You sign up at the visitor center and then you get a specific designated location. The hikes can last between one and a half to two and a half hours– they are moderately strenuous at one to two miles in length.

Winter in Bryce Canyon is a unique adventure in itself, and going on a guided snowshoe hike is a wonderful experience. You'll learn about the geology of the park and how it is impacted in the winter months.

ZION

If you are going to spend a couple days in Zion, there are two main areas of the park you need to explore: the Narrows and Kolob Canyons. Of course, there is plenty more to see in the park so you should consider coming back later for a longer trip.

THE NARROWS

The Narrows is one of the most visited sections of Zion National Park, as well as the narrowest section of the main Zion Canyon. The walls are 1,000 feet tall and the river is sometimes no more than 20 to 30 feet wide. You can get to the

Narrows by hiking the paved wheelchair-accessible trail from Riverside Walk for a mile, or you can get to it from the Temple of Sinawava.

If you want to go further into the Narrows, you will need to walk in the Virgin River, which involves some wading upstreaming for a few minutes– alternatively, you can turn it into an all-day hike.

The best time to hike the Narrows is in late spring and summer when the water is both at its lowest and warmest. However, keep in mind that this is also the time of year when storms are most likely to cause flash floods. You can still hike the Narrows during the winter and early spring, but the water levels are going to be higher and the water can be colder.

If the snowmelt raises the river over 150 CFS (cubic feet per second), the Narrows can be closed in the spring. Fall offers more stable weather, but the days are shorter and the water temperature is lower.

The water level varies greatly throughout the year depending on a range of factors, including rainfall and snowmelt. If the water level is below 70 CFS, walking can be moderately difficult. You'll be doing knee-deep crossings on a slippery and uneven river bottom with frequent pools that are up to your waist.

Once the level is over 70 CFS, walking against the current is challenging as mid-thigh deep water and pools can be chest-deep. When the flow is over 150 CFS, the Narrows is closed to all traffic. It will also close when a Flash Flood Warning is issued by the National Weather Service, and will continue to be closed until two hours after an alert is lifted.

During a flash flood, water levels can rise nearly instantly within seconds or minutes. These have been known to strand, injure, and even kill those who venture into the Narrows and other flood-prone canyons. Always check the weather before heading into any destination that is mainly covered in bare rock, as it will not absorb the water and will become dangerous during heavy rainfall.

Kolob Canyons

The Kolob Canyons are a part of Zion National Park off Interstate 15, Exit 40 about 40 miles north of Zion Canyon and 17 miles south of Cedar City. Take a five-mile scenic drive along the Kolob Canyons Road to view the crimson canyons and stop to access numerous trails and scenic viewpoints.

Kolob Canyons is located in the northwest corner of the park and is a series of narrow parallel box canyons in the western edge of the Colorado Plateau with 2,000 foot cliff walls. You can stop to view panoramic vistas on your scenic drive, hike a canyon, or set off on a multi-day wilderness adventure. There is something for everyone to experience in Kolob Canyons.

When visiting you need to stop at the Visitor Center and provide an Interagency Park Pass or pay an entrance fee. You can also get wilderness permits for backpacking campsites and canyoneering routes.

Kolob Canyons are a designated wilderness area that is protected because of their primitive environments. This is a quieter section of the park when you want to escape from the crowds.

These canyons are a place for solitude and tranquility with over 20 miles of hiking trails available for peaceful exploration and roaming as one ponders about anything they might have been troubled by. In other words, there are very few problems whose answers are not found after a long walk at Kolob Canyons.

PART – 4

A DETAIL IN-DEPTH LOOK INSIDE 7 MOST POPULAR PARKS

IN –DEPTH GUIDE TO ARCHES, BRYCE CANYON, GRAND TETON, YELLOWSTONE, ZION, ROCKY MOUNTAIN & GLACIER NATIONAL PARKS

IN-DEPTH GUIDE TO ARCHES NATIONAL PARK

We've already discussed a few of the activities one may participate in at Arches National Park, but let's take an in-depth look at everything else you can see and do during an extended stay.

ACTIVITIES

- ☐ Scenic Driving
- ☐ Backpacking
- ☐ Biking
- ☐ Camping
- ☐ Canyoneering
- ☐ Commercial Tours
- ☐ Hiking
- ☐ Horseback Riding
- ☐ Photography
- ☐ Ranger Guided Tours
- ☐ Rock Climbing
- ☐ Stargazing

BACKPACKING

The backcountry of Arches National Park is rough and often inaccessible by established trails and limited water. Arches is home to geologic features, cultural resources, and sensitive high desert ecosystems. There are rare water sources in the area, so you need to carry all the water you need.

Your main safety concerns are steep terrain, loose rocks, lightning, flash floods, and dehydration. You'll also want to be familiar with all park regulations before exploring it without any prior knowledge.

PERMITS

Any overnight stay in the backcountry will require a permit. Permits are only issued in person at the Arches Visitor Center up to seven days before the trip start and up to an hour before closing. A single permit is good for a maximum amount of seven people, and three nights per campsite or zone for a maximum of seven nights. They cost $7 per person.

REQUIREMENTS

Any use of the backcountry and vehicle access is done at your own risk. You'll need to plan ahead and prepare for the conditions you are likely to face. There are some routes that aren't marked.

You are required to carry a commercial toilet bag system with you. These will render solid human waste into a non-hazardous material and must be packed out with you. These bags cannot be disposed of in toilets. There is a specific container at the camp host site in Devils Garden campground where you can dispose of these bags.

Courthouse Wash and Lost Spring Canyon are active flowing areas that can be unpredictable. When camping in a dry wash use caution and never attempt to cross a wash when there are flood conditions.

You must know and follow all park rules and regulations when it comes to backcountry use, including the following:
- ☐ Wood campfires are prohibited.

- ☐ Food must be stored securely to prevent animals from accessing it.
- ☐ All trash must be packed out at the end of your trip.
- ☐ Swimming, bathing, or immersing yourself in water is only allowed where there is a continuous supply of water.
- ☐ All camping activities must be within designated campsite boundaries and within the boundaries of at-large zones. Campsites must be vacated at 10am.
- ☐ When camping in a zone you must be:

  - ☐ A minimum of one mile away from main roads
  - ☐ A minimum of a half mile away from any trails
  - ☐ A minimum of 300 feet away from archeological sites.
  - ☐ A minimum of 300 feet away from non-flowing water sources.
  - ☐ You must stay in low impact areas such as slickrock and be established before sunset.

- ☐ You must protect all natural plants, objects, and cultural artifacts by leaving them where they are found. You cannot touch rock art or draw graffiti.
- ☐ Prohibited actions include bringing pets, discharging firearms, hunting, and feeding wildlife.

SAFETY

Safety is not guaranteed by the park so you need to make safety your primary responsibility. Consider the following to stay safe in the backcountry:

- ☐ Check the weather constantly.
- ☐ During a thunderstorm, lightning is a serious concern so take refuge in a safe area as soon as possible.
- ☐ Climbing up slickrock is easier than going down.

- ☐ Never feed the wildlife.
- ☐ Plan and know your route in advance.
- ☐ Be prepared to rescue yourself if needed.

BACKCOUNTRY CAMPING

Camping in designated sites and zones while in the backcountry will result in minimal impact to park resources. This also makes it easier for you to select a site and allow you to better enjoy your experience. The following are the available backcountry sites in Arches National Park.

Site/Zone	Campsites	Area
Courthouse Wash	3 campsites: 2 in Upper Courthouse Wash 1 in Lower Courthouse Wash	A wash bottom with dense brush. Navigation skills are required.
Devil's Garden	1 campsite	Located off Devils Garden Primitive Trail

BIKING

Biking is allowed inside the park on all paved and unpaved roads. Biking is not allowed on trails or anywhere off a road, however. The Salt Valley and Willow Springs Roads are less traveled, but these dirt roads consist of washboards, deep sand, and other obstacles, so mountain bikes are better suited for the job.

CANYONEERING

Canyoneering is an activity that requires climbing equipment to make technical descents into and through canyons. While there aren't a lot of slot canyons at Arches National Park, it does have a number of narrow passages cross-hatched into the sandstone walls to make canyoneering one of your outdoor exploration options.

In 2013, the park developed a Climbing and Canyoneering Management Plan to protect the natural environment of the park while improving visitor experiences. The plan included the implementation of size limits, canyoneer registration, education, safety standards, and routes for access and egress.

REGULATIONS

Unless you plan to canyoneer in the Fiery Furnace, you will need to complete a free self-registration permit to canyoneer in designated areas of Arches National Park.

Canyoneering in the Fiery Furnace or Lost Spring Canyon is limited to a maximum of six people. All other canyoneering groups are limited to ten people. Larger groups need to split up and use different routes or use the same route at different times throughout the day to avoid queuing at rappel sites and to minimize the impact on park visitors and resources.

You are not allowed to climb, scramble, or walk on any named or unnamed arch with an opening of over three feet. You are also not allowed to wrap webbing or rope around any of these arches for the purpose of rappelling or climbing.

You are also prohibited from physically altering the natural position of rocks through chiseling, breaking rocks to reinforce crevices and pockets as anchors, glue reinforcement of existing holds and gluing of new holds. Along with this you cannot intentionally remove lichen or plants from rock.

You cannot bathe or immerse yourself in water sources that don't have a regular flow both in and out at the time of activity, except in cases when it is necessary to traverse a route.

The use of Deadman anchors is not allowed. Installing pitons is also prohibited.

You need to obtain a permit in order to install new fixed gear. If an existing item or fixed anchor is unsafe, it may be replaced without a permit.

Any software left behind needs to match the rock surface in color. Before installing any bolts, hangers, and chains you need to paint them the color of the rock.

Using a motorized drill is prohibited within wilderness areas and requires a special use permit.

The activities of guided canyoneering, slacklining, and highlining are prohibited.

REGISTRATION

In order to canyoneer in Arches National Park you need to register and obtain a free permit. There are no daily limits on any routes other than the Fiery Furnace, which means you can get a permit on the day of the trip. Registration is free, helps with your safety, and allows the park to maintain desired conditions while in the backcountry.

You can obtain permits from the online reservation system of the park or by self-registration at the kiosk outside the visitor center. If you want to canyoneer in the Fiery Furnace, your entire group needs to come to the front desk at the visitor center to get a permit at $6 a person. Permits are limited to 75 people a day and are often sold out during busy seasons.

SAFETY

The park doesn't guarantee safety while canyoneering, so safety is your own responsibility– this point cannot be reiterated enough times. It is important that you take an honest assessment of your skill level and limitations when it comes to the risks of canyoneering.

Don't attempt any routes that are beyond your abilities or those of anyone in your group. Keep the following in mind when it comes to canyoneering safely:

- ☐ Check the weather beforehand and during your hike.
- ☐ Research routes and know your chosen path well.
- ☐ Inspect all fixed gear carefully, especially webbing knots.
- ☐ Be ready to rescue yourself if needed.
- ☐ Any significant hazards and injuries should be reported to a park ranger.

CANYONEERING ROUTES

There are several established routes in the park that are approved for canyoneering. You will need a special use permit in order to establish other canyoneering routes with fixed gear.

Area	Route
Fiery Furnace	Krill Lomatium
Great Wall	Bighorn
Lost Spring Canyon	Lost and Found Undercover MMI
Park Avenue	Tierdrop Not Tierdrop U-Turn
Petrified Dunes	Dragonfly

The Windows	Elephant Butte

COMMERCIAL TOURS

If you prefer a more guided approach, consider a commercial tour to help get you around the park while learning about the area. There are several companies that have concession contracts with the park service to conduct 4WD tours of the park.

1. Adrift Adventures
2. NAVTEC Expeditions
3. OARS

There are other commercial activities you can do, including guided van tours and hikes. A lot of companies offer shuttle service to the visitor center as well as trailheads within the park. You can contact the Moab Travel Council for a full list of companies that offer this service.

HIKING

There are several hiking opportunities within Arches National Park, ranging from easy to strenuous. Let's look at all your hiking options:

EASY HIKES

- ☐ Balanced Rock, 0.3 miles
- ☐ The Windows, 1 mile
- ☐ Double Arch, 0.5 miles
- ☐ Delicate Arch Viewpoints, 100 yard and 0.5 miles
- ☐ Sand Dune Arch, 0.3 miles

- ☐ Broken Arch Loop, 2 miles
- ☐ Skyline Arch, 0.4 miles
- ☐ Landscape Arch at Devils Garden, 1.6 miles
- ☐ Courthouse Arch Rock Art, 1 mile

MODERATE HIKES

- ☐ Park Avenue, 2 miles

STRENUOUS HIKES

- ☐ Tower Arch, 3.4 miles
- ☐ Delicate Arch, 3 miles
- ☐ Double O Arch at Devils Garden, 4.5 miles
- ☐ Primitive Trail at Devils Garden, 7.2 miles
- ☐ Fiery Furnace

HORSEBACK RIDING

If you prefer to explore the outdoors by horse, then you'll love the horseback riding option at Arches National Park. While horses are permitted in the park, there are some restrictions on where they can go and how they can be maneuvered.

Horseback riding as well as the use of a pack animal is restricted to day use only.

Park animals are designated as horses, mules, and burros. No other animals can be used as pack animals, including llamas and goats.

Using saddle or pack animals is permitted in the following areas:

- Salt Wash upstream from the Delicate Arch Road
- Courthouse Wash
- Seven Mile Canyon

Travel in road less areas is restricted to wash bottoms with the exception of leaving to avoid quicksand.

Horses and pack animals are allowed on all designated 4WD roads within the park. They are also allowed on the following 2WD roads and non-paved roads:

- Salt Valley Road from the main park road to the west boundary of the park.
- Klondike Bluffs Road

The maximum size allowed is 10 people and 10 pack animals.

If possible, horses should be watered downstream from a source. Any manure that is dropped in or near a spring or non-flowing water source needs to be removed immediately in order to avoid contamination. Any manure spilled from a trailering unit along with feed needs to be picked up before departing.

You should attempt to picket your horses in a location that has the least amount of damage from vegetation. Animals can't be tied to trees or other vegetation directly except for the salt cedar plant.

Grazing or loose herding is not allowed and you are required to carry feed for overnight trips. When traveling in the backcountry, you are prohibited from using loose hay or grain containing viable seeds. You are required to carry supplemental weed-free feed.

Any commercial guiding trips need to be provided by an outfitter who is authorized to operate under commercial use procedures within the park.

Rock Climbing

The rock formations at Arches National Park provide ample opportunities for climbing despite the sandy nature of the soil. Most of the climbing routes in the park require advanced techniques.

Regulations

Rock climbing within the park is limited to five persons per group.

Rock climbing must be free or clean aid climbing. Slacklining, highlining, and base jumping are prohibited. You are prohibited from installing pitons, using white chalk or motorized drills.

You cannot alter rocks from their natural positions by chiseling, breaking rocks to reinforce crevices and pockets as anchors, gluing reinforcements and gluing new holds. You also cannot intentionally remove or "garden" lichen or plants from any stones.

Existing items or fixed anchors may be replaced if they are unsafe. Any replacements need to be painted the color of the rock surface or primered brown. Fixed ropes are not to be left in place for more than 24 hours unless you notify the park.

In order to bivvy overnight you will need a backcountry permit and you need to follow the rules and regulations for backcountry camping. Bivvying needs to be at least a mile from a designated road and a half mile from a designated trail.

Registration

If you are planning to do some rock climbing in the park, you should register by getting a free permit. There are no daily limits on routes, so you can get your permit on the day if you plan to climb.

Registration is free and it helps keep you safe while allowing the park to maintain desired conditions. You can get a permit through the park's online registration system or you can self-register at the kiosk at the visitor center.

Safety

The park cannot guarantee your safety while rock climbing, so you need to make safety your primary responsibility. Know the dangers of rock climbing and take care of yourself during your chosen activities. Consider the following to have a safe experience:

- ☐ Check the weather.
- ☐ Research your route.
- ☐ Inspect all fixed gear before using.
- ☐ Be prepared to rescue yourself.

Rock Climbing Routes

Park Area	Route	Closure Dates
Arches Entrance	The Pickle	April 1st to August 31st
Arches Switchbacks	The Three Penguins	March 1st to August 15th
Devils Garden & Devil Dog Spire	Industrial Disease	December 1st to September 30th
Garden of Eden & Ham Rock	Harkonnen Castle	March 15th to August 15th
Highway 191	Canyonlands by Night	March 1st to August 31st

	El Secondo The Coup	
Highway 191 & Crohn's Wall	Left Route Crohn's Odyssey Project One Project Two	March 1st to August 31st
Klondike Bluffs	Klondike Bluffs Crack	March 1st to August 31st
Klondike Bluffs & The Bouquet	Route One Route Two	March 1st to August 31st
Klondike Bluffs & Marching Men	Cuddle Bunny Tower False Start North Marcher	March 1st to August 31st
Highway 128 & Goose Island	Fun Ramp The Hyena Trail of the Navajo	March 1st to August 31st
Highway 128 & Milano Tower	Pop Tarts	March 1st to August 31st
Highway 128	Escape Route	March 1st to August 31st
Windows & Tonka Tower	Tonka Tower	March 15th to August 15th

IN-DEPTH GUIDE TO BRYCE CANYON NATIONAL PARK

There is a lot to see and do at Bryce Canyon National Park depending on your personal preferences. You may even want to return several times throughout the year to enjoy every part of the park.

There are three wonderful festivals you can take delight in throughout the year and there are lots of hiking options. Let's look at each of these in greater detail so you can plan how long you need to spend at this national park.

FESTIVALS

GEOLOGY FESTIVAL

Usually scheduled in July, this festival is great for those who want to learn and know more about the natural geology found in the park. During this festival you can join ranger-guided hikes, family-focused geology programs, bus tours with a geologist, evening programs featuring guest speakers, special exhibits at the visitor center, and family-oriented activities.

PRAIRIE DOG FESTIVAL

Often held in April, this focus is on the native prairie dog. In addition to visiting local schools to teach about this species, park rangers also host informative talks at the park. This is the peak time to visit the park and catch a glimpse of these quirky, robust little animals.

ASTRONOMY FESTIVAL

Typically held in June, this festival offers unique astronomy events and special speakers. For those who want a unique stargazing experience and to learn more about our vast skies, this is the event to attend.

HIKING TRAILS

Most of the hiking in Bryce Canyon consists of smaller trails that interconnect. This allows you to connect as many routes as you want and to make your hiking experience as long and as difficult as you wish. Let's look at the hiking options you have while staying at this park.

EASY HIKING TRAILS

MOSSY CAVE

This is a short 0.8-mile round-trip hike. It is located outside of the amphitheater along Highway 12 toward Tropic. This hike is a streamside walk to a mossy overhang and small waterfall. The water typically flows from May to October.

As you hike up the trail, take the left fork to reach Mossy Cave. This is more of a shelter cave. Depending on the season, you'll either see a overhang filled with moss or giant icicles. Mossy Cave is defined as a grotto that was created by an underground spring.

If you take the right fork of the trail you'll reach a small waterfall. Here you'll see an example of Dolomite, a special type of limestone fortified by magnesium. Dolomite is responsible for creating this waterfall and is the caprock that you typically see on the hoodoos in the area.

Rim Trail

This hike is an 11-mile round-trip and includes Sunset Point to Sunrise Point Trail at an additional one-mile round-trip. Here you can observe the amphitheater and the hoodoos along the rim. Plan your visit to include all four main viewpoints.

Bristlecone Loop

This hike is a short one-mile round-trip. It takes you through spruce forests,, cliffs covered with bristlecone pines, and breathtaking vistas. It is reached from Rainbow Point at the southern end of the park and reaches an elevation of over 9,100 feet. You'll see various bird species on your hike including grouse, woodpeckers, and owls. This trail is often inaccessible in mid-winter due to high snow levels.

Queens Garden

This hike is a 1.8-mile round-trip and is the easiest hike. The trail commences at Sunrise Point and guides you down 320 feet into the canyon. The many hoodoos in the area make you feel as if you are hiking in a garden.

Moderate Hiking Trails

Navajo Trail

Here we are looking at a 1.3-mile round-trip hike. It starts at Sunset Point and takes you into the Bryce Amphitheater via a slot canyon. This is one of the more popular hikes in the park and can be combined with the easy Queens Garden hike. Be aware that rock slides are frequent on this trail and there are a lot of loose rocks.

Tower Bridge

This hike consists of a three-mile round-trip that begins at Sunset Point and leads you northeast along the Fairyland Loop Trail. It is considered a moderate hike due to the drop in elevation down to the Tower Bridge site. Allow about two to three hours to complete the trip.

Once you reach the Tower Bridge you can either return to Sunset Point or you can continue on the Fairyland Loop for a total of eight miles. Be aware that snakes and other animals are common on this trail. You should carry plenty of water and have sun protection as well as hiking boots and long pants.

Hat Shop

This hike is four-mile round-trip which begins at Bryce Point and is a down and back trail. Walk along the Under the Rim Trail and come to a cluster of hoodoos known as Hat Shop.

The trail features a steep descent, so those with knee issues should avoid it entirely. During the winter, this route is very difficult and shouldn't be attempted without advanced planning.

Swamp Canyon

This hike is a 4.3-mile round-trip. The canyon is small and features lots of fins and hoodoos on both sides. It is an excellent way to get an up close view of the landscape and geology of the area. From the Swamp Canyon overlook you can descend to the Under the Rim Trail and make a loop to return to the other side.

It is best to start in the clockwise direction. While this hike is moderate, it can easily become difficult if you aren't prepared. Plan and pack accordingly. Spring and summer see an abundance of bees on the trail due to flowering sweet-scented plants.

STRENUOUS HIKING TRAILS

FAIRYLAND LOOP

This hike is eight-miles long and starts at Fairyland Point at the northern portion of the park. It walks you along the rim and into the canyon. There is a spur trail that takes you to Tower Bridge. The trail is strenuous due to its length and numerous elevation changes.

A portion of the loop includes the Rim Trail from Sunset Point to Fairyland Point. It typically takes four to five hours to hike and it is recommended to carry at least one quart of water for each two to three hours of hiking per person. Sunscreen and hats are recommended in the summer. Be aware of snakes.

PEEK-A-BOO LOOP

The loop is a 5.5-mile round-trip. It is first seen at Bryce Point and quickly drops to the canyon floor. Both the length and rapid elevation change makes it a strenuous hike. Be prepared to encounter horse and mule riders on this trail, and give them right of way if encountered. There are restrooms available at the bottom. Wear proper shoes since ankle injuries are common.

RIGGS SPRING LOOP

Another loop that consists of an 8.5-mile round-trip. The trail starts at Yovimpa Point and takes you through a forest with spruce, fir, and bristlecone trees. On the eastern side you'll see red cliff breaks and quaking aspen groves. To the east and south you'll be able to see beautiful vistas.

The western section of the trail is steeper, with denser forests. Near the midway point you'll come to a spring, which offers a great shady spot to stop and rest if needed. Be sure to treat the water before drinking. This area is a popular backcountry camping area.

IN-DEPTH GUIDE TO ZION NATIONAL PARK

Zion National Park was the first in Utah and is a major destination for outdoor enthusiasts. You can easily spend a week at this park and probably still have plenty more to see and do. Let's look at all the activities available so you can plan how many days you need to see all you want to see.

ACTIVITIES

- ☐ Backpacking
- ☐ Bicycling
- ☐ Birding
- ☐ Camping
- ☐ Canyoneering
- ☐ Climbing
- ☐ Hiking
- ☐ Horseback Riding
- ☐ Ranger Guided Activities
- ☐ River Trips
- ☐ Stock Use
- ☐ Sunset and Stargazing

BACKPACKING TRAIL OPTIONS

In addition to the popular hiking areas of the park, Zion National Park is also home to several wonderful backpacking experiences. Let's look at the backpacking trail options you have available during your visit.

EAST RIM TRAIL

Covers East Entrance Trailhead to Weeping Rock at a distance of 10.8 miles. There is a seasonal water source at Stave Spring. The trail is open in spring and fall. You can access it from either East Entrance Trailhead or Weeping Rock Trailhead. From this trail you can also branch off to East Mesa, Deertrap, and Cable Mountain.

If you start from the East Entrance Trailhead you will need to climb 1,000 feet to the rim with views of Jolley Gulch and the slickrock areas on the east side. Next, you hike through a ponderosa forest. After crossing the rim, you could appreciate views of Echo Canyon Basin. Once you hike over the rim of the canyon you will quickly descend 2,300 feet to the floor of Zion Canyon and end at Weeping Rock.

Along the way, pass through Echo Canyon and down the Observation Point Trail. There are no established campsites in the area, but you do need a permit for overnight camping.

Hop Valley Trail

Covers Hop Valley Trailhead to La Verkin Creek at a distance of 6.5 miles– it is available in the spring, summer, and fall, and is accessed from the Hop Valley Railhead. There is no water source on this trail, so come prepared with your own containers of water.

Along the way, you can access La Verkin Creek, Kolob Arch, and the Connector Trail. The trail starts off Kolob Terrace Road, takes you through open fields with views of the nearby rock formations, and descends as you get near Hop Valley. On the valley floor, the path is sandy and well-worn. Campsites are located at the far end of the valley before the steep descent starts into La Verkin Creek. You are only allowed to camp in designated sites.

LA VERKIN CREEK TRAIL

Covers Lee Pass to Kolob Arch at a distance of seven miles, and Kolob Arch to Hop Valley Trailhead at a distance of 7.4 miles– the trail is accessible from Lee Pass. It is available during the spring, summer, and fall. There are water sources at Beatty Spring and La Verkin Creek. The trail takes you by open canyons as it follows Timber Creek. Once you get within view of La Verkin Creek, the trail slopes down to the creek bottom on a hard-packed trail.

Once you reach the creek bed, the trail starts upstream with panoramas of the surrounding cliffs. You will travel seven miles to one of the main destinations on this trail, the aforementioned Kolob Arch. From here, you can continue on to Bear Trap Canyon and Willis Canyon to extend your trip. This is a great hike to bask in over the course of a few days, but you can only camp in designated sites.

SOUTHWEST DESERT (CHINLE TRAIL AND COALPITS WASH)

From Chinle Trailhead to Coalpits Wash, the distance is 8.1 miles; from the Coalpits Trailhead to Chinle Trail, the distance is 3.6 miles. There are water sources at the Coalpits Spring and Coalpits Wash seasonally. The trail is open in the fall, winter, and spring, and starts at the Anasazi Way Subdivision.

There are more paths found at Coalpits Trailhead and Chinle Trailhead. This location takes you across open desert as it heads towards the base of Mount Kinesava. It also crosses an area of petrified wood and cryptobiotic soil. In the summer, the trail can be very hot, but it feels very pleasant in the spring and fall.

There is no developed trail in Coalpits Wash, but there is an easy-to-follow, well-beaten path that leads you to the junction with Scoggins Wash. At this junction, you should stay left and head up the canyon pass boulders and small waterfalls. There is camping in designated sites only.

THE NARROWS AT THE NORTH FORK OF THE VIRGIN RIVER

There are 16 miles from Chamberlain's Ranch to the Temple of Sinawava. There are water sources at the Virgin River and Big Spring. The trail is open in the summer and fall. There are trailheads at Chamberlain's Ranch and the Temple of Sinawava.

This is an unforgettable wilderness hiking experience, but this isn't an easy hike to be undertaken by everyone. Part of this hike entails hiking in the Virgin River, and nearly 80% of the hike is spent wading, walking, and even swimming in the river.

There is no maintained trail, but you simply follow the river. The current can sometimes be swift with very cold water, so you face danger from hypothermia and flash flooding. You'll need good planning, proper equipment, and excellent judgement before heading out on this hike. You are only allowed to camp in designated sites.

WEST RIM TRAIL

Covers West Rim Trailhead to the Grotto at a distance of 14.2 miles by the Rim Trail and 13.6 miles by the Telephone Canyon Trail. There are seasonal water sources at Sawmill Springs and Potato Hollow Spring, with Cabin Spring available all year. The trail is open late spring, summer, and fall.

If you are starting at the West Rim Trailhead near Lava Point, you can cross the high alpine elevation and delve into the Wildcat Canyon area that takes the first 6.5 miles then drops you into Potato Hollow. The trail climbs out of the hollow and splits into the Telephone Canyon Trail and the West Rim Trail.

The West Rim Trail traces along the rim to views of Phantom Valley and the canyons to the south. The Telephone Canyon Trail provides a shortcut from Potato Hollow to Cabin Spring, or a loop if you want to enter and exit the same trailhead. At Cabin Spring, the trail takes a steep drop of 2,500 feet in 4.7 miles to end at the Grotto Picnic Area. You are only allowed to camp in designated sites.

Wildcat Canyon Trail

This trail covers the route from Wildcat Trailhead to the West Rim Trail at a distance of 5.8 miles, and it is open throughout late spring, summer, and fall. There is a water source at Wildcat Spring, as well as trailheads at Wildcat Trailhead and West Rim Trailhead.

The Wildcat Trailhead leads you past the Northgate Peaks Trail Junction and comes along with views of the Northgate Peaks as it all goes through a ponderosa pine forest. The trail then opens to meadows before reaching the edge of Wildcat Canyon with a deep overlook into the canyon.

Once you cross that section, there will be a slight climb until everything connects with the West Rim Trail. There are no established campsites in this area, but a permit is needed for overnight camping.

Hiking

Easy Trails

- ☐ Pa'rus Trail, 3.5-mile round-trip – 2 hours
- ☐ Archeology Trail, 0.4-mile round-trip – half hour
- ☐ Lower Emerald Pool Trail, 1.2-mile round-trip – 1 hour
- ☐ The Grotto Trail, 1 mile round-trip – half hour

- ☐ Weeping Rock Trail, 0.4-mile round-trip – half hour
- ☐ Riverside Walk, 2.2-mile round-trip – 1 and ½ hours

Moderate Trails

- ☐ Watchman Trail, 3.3-mile round-trip – 2 hours
- ☐ Sand Bench Trail, 7.6-mile round-trip – 5 hours
- ☐ Upper Emerald Pool Trail 1 mile round trip – 1 hour
- ☐ Kayenta Trail, 2-miles round-trip – 1 and ½ hours
- ☐ Canyon Overlook Trail, 1-mile round-trip – 1 hour
- ☐ Taylor Creek Trail, 5-mile round-trip – 3 and ½ hours
- ☐ Timber Creek Overlook Trail, 1-mile round-trip – half hour

Strenuous Trails

- ☐ Angels Landing via West Rim Trail, 5.4-mile round-trip – 4 hours
- ☐ Hidden Canyon Trail, 2.4-mile round trip – 2 and ½ hours
- ☐ Observation Point via East Rim Trail, 8-mile round-trip – 6 hours
- ☐ The Narrows via Riverside Walk, 9.4-mile round trip – Up to 8 hours
- ☐ Kolob Arch via La Verkin Creek Trail, 14-mile round-trip – 8 hours

IN-DEPTH GUIDE TO ROCKY MOUNTAIN NATIONAL PARK

It would take several days to see all the areas of Rocky Mountain National Park and even then you may need to take several trips in order to hike all the trails and take part in all the outdoor activities offered.

Let's look at a seven-day trip to the park that would allow you to see and do the most.

A Week in Rocky Mountain

Day One

Start your trip with an easy hike on a short trail to stretch your legs and get used to the surrounding. Maybe consider a lake or embarking on a waterfall hike. Often, people need a day or two to get used to the altitude at this park. So, it may be a good idea to stay at the lower elevations at first.

Day Two

If you are getting more comfortable with the elevation, take a trip into the higher country by car. Trail Ridge Road is a great option since it has many excellent scenic overlooks of the park. Take a leisurely day-long drive with short hikes and maybe listen to a ranger talk to get used to the region.

Day Three

Start your day with a ranger-guided birding tour. Even if you aren't that into birds, this can be an informative and interesting activity. Spend the rest of your day taking a slightly longer hike with a picnic stop for lunch. Some great options are the hikes along Big Thompson River.

Day Four

Go on a hike into the backcountry. Consider the options and choose one suited to your physical ability and regional preferences.

Day Five

Participate in a class offered by the Rocky Mountain Conservancy Field Institute. These classes can last for a half-day, full-day, or multi-day depending on your physical ability. They cover a range of subjects such as nature and cultural history. Choose from subjects such as outdoor skills, photography, wildlife, art, and/or history.

Day Six

By now you should be better acclimated to the elevation. You can head out on a more strenuous hike. A popular option is high country lakes. This is a good time to apply what you've learned over the last five days outdoors.

Day Seven

Now's the chance to try something new. Consider horseback riding, fishing, climbing, or some other activity within your physical means that you haven't done before. After this you'll really know there's a lot more to do and you'll be planning your next trip back to the park in no time.

HIKING

Lake Hiking Chart

Trailhead	Destination	Distance
Bear Lake	Nymph Lake	0.5 miles
A great hike for those new to the park.		
Bear Lake	Dream Lake	1.1 miles
A short climb with rewarding views.		
Bierstadt Lake Bear Lake	Bierstadt Lake	1.4 miles 1.6 miles
A mountain hike through dense forest.		
Fern Lake	The Pool	1.7 miles
A peaceful hike along Big Thompson River.		
Bear Lake	Emerald Lake	1.8 miles
A popular destination at the base of the mountains.		
Lumpy Ridge	Gem Lake	1.8 miles
A year-round hike to a beautiful lake.		
Bear Lake	Lake Haiyaha	2.1 miles
A lake surrounded by the Continental Divide.		
Cub Lake	Cub Lake	2.3 miles
A beautiful trail with summer wildflowers.		
Glacier Gorge	Mills Lake	2.8 miles
A lake surrounded by mountain scenery.		
Glacier Gorge	The Loch	3 miles

A lake in a mountain setting.		
Fern Lake	Fern Lake	3.8 miles
The shoreline was once home to a lodge.		
Bear Lake Fern Lake	Odessa Lake	4.1 miles 4.4 miles
A mountain lake at the base of the peaks.		
Longs Peak	Chasm Lake	4.2 miles
Rugged lake home to marmots.		
Sandbeach Lake	Sandbeach Lake	4.2 miles
A steady climb rewarded by magnificent sights.		
Finch Lake	Finch Lake	4.5 miles
A moderate climb through the remains of the 1978 fire.		
Glacier Gorge	Sky Pond	4.9 miles
A climb up the Continental Divide.		
Glacier Gorge	Black Lake	5 miles
A mountain hike above Ribbon Falls.		
East Inlet	Lone Pine Lake	5.5 miles
A strenuous hike to a lake with sheer rock cliffs.		
Wild Basin	Bluebird Lake	6 miles
A moderate southeastern hike with wildflowers.		
Finch Lake	Pear Lake	6.5 miles
Strenuous hike to a remote location.		
Wild Basin	Thunder Lake	6.8 miles

A high elevation hike to a lake with a meadow.		
East Inlet	Lake Verna	6.9 miles
Strenuous hike to a fjord-like lake.		
Wild Basin	Lion Lake No. 1	7 miles
A subalpine lake with wildflowers.		
East Inlet	Spirit Lake	7.8 miles
Moderate hike to the west side of the lake for remote fishing.		
North Inlet	Lake Nokoni	9.9 miles
A strenuous hike to a distant lake.		
North Inlet	Lake Nanita	11 miles
A strenuous hike through the park's interior.		

Waterfall Hiking Chart

Trailhead	Destination	Distance
Wild Basin	Copeland Falls	0.3 miles
An ideal hike for families.		
Glacier Gorge Bear Lake	Alberta Falls	0.8 miles 0.9 miles
An easy hike to a popular park destination.		
Wild Basin	Calypso Cascades	1.8 miles
Easy hike to a waterfall with the Calypso Orchid.		
Fern Lake	Fern Falls	2.7 miles
An easy hike to a refreshing rest place.		

Wild Basin	Ouzel Falls	2.7 miles
An easy hike to a popular destination.		
North Inlet	Cascade Falls	3.5 miles
An easy hike through a forest.		
Glacier Gorge	Timberline Falls	4 miles
A moderate climb to wonderful views.		

Mountain Summits Hiking Chart

Trailhead	Destination	Distance/Height
Deer Mountain	Deer Mountain	3 miles/10,013 feet
Strenuous hike with a good picnic destination.		
Alpine VC	Alpine Ridge Trail	0.5 miles/11,428 feet
Short hike to an overlook.		
Bear Lake	Flattop Mountain	4.4 miles/12,324 feet
Strenuous climb to panoramic views and access to other summits.		
Lily Lake	Estes Cone	3.7 miles/11,006 feet
Strenuous hike to some of the best vistas in the park.		

IN-DEPTH GUIDE TO YELLOWSTONE NATIONAL PARK

One of the highlights of visiting Yellowstone National Park is the eruption of the Old Faithful Geyser. However, there are numerous other things to see and do in the park. You can easily spend an entire trip in just one portion of the park, so let's look at that list, shall we?

FISHING BRIDGE, LAKE VILLAGE, AND BRIDGE BAY AREA

VIEW FISH AT FISHING BRIDGE

The original bridge at this site was built in 1902 from rough-hewn corduroy logs. The current bridge was built in 1937. Historically, this has always been a popular fishing destination since it was a major spawning spot for the cutthroat trout.

Since the cutthroat population has declined, the bridge was closed to fishing practices in 1973. In turn, the place is now more of an observation point for viewing the fish instead.

YELLOWSTONE LAKE

Geologists have discovered that a large volcanic eruption occurs about every 600,000 years. The last eruption occurred from two large vents near Old Faithful, the Mallard Lake Dome, and another north of Fishing Bridge, the Sour Creek Dome.

The magma chamber then collapsed, leading to the formation of a large caldera filled with lava flow. Part of the caldera is now the 136-mile Basin of Yellowstone

Lake. Originally, the lake was 200 feet higher than it is now. Be sure to visit this lake and walk around the shoreline.

VISIT THE MUD VOLCANO

The Mud Volcano and Sulphur Caldron are primary spots for the thermal features known as mud pots and fumaroles. This is because both are located on a water system with little water actually available. Fumaroles or "steam vents" occur when the ground water boils away faster than it has the ability to recharge.

The vapors are high in sulfuric acid which leaches into the rock and turns it into clay. Since there is no water to wash away the leached rock or acid, it forms a mud pot. Steam and gases explode through the layers of mud, making it a widely unstable region to visit without the proper guidance.

WILDLIFE VIEWING IN HAYDEN AND PELICAN VALLEYS

Located six miles north of Fishing Bridge Junction you'll find Hayden Valley while Pelican Valley is just three miles east of Fishing Bridge. These two valleys make up some of the best habitats for wildlife in the lower 48 states such as grizzly bears, bison, elk, and other species. The Hayden Valley was formed by an arm of Yellowstone Lake.

HIKE TO NATURAL BRIDGE

From the Bridge Bay Campground this is an easy one-mile hike. There is also a bicycle trail that will bring you to the Natural Bridge. The top of the bridge is about 51 feet above the creek. You can take a short switchback trail to the top, but traveling across the bridge is prohibited in order to preserve and protect the structure.

Canyon Village

Hike to Artist's Point

From Upper Falls to the Tower Fall area, the Grand Canyon of Yellowstone is about 20 miles long. The canyon was formed as the Yellowstone River flowed and eroded the area. The Upper Falls is 109 feet high and can be seen from the Brink of the Upper Falls Trail and Uncle Tom's Trail.

The Lower Falls is 308 feet high and can be viewed from Lookout Point, Red Rock Point, Artist Point, Brink of the Lower Falls Trail, and numerous points along the South Rim Trail.

Wildlife Viewing in Hayden Valley

A great place to observe wildlife is the Hayden Valley. In the spring and early summer you are likely to see grizzly bears as they hunt newborn bison and elk calves. At the same time you'll also catch a glimpse of large herds of bison. Coyotes are also commonly seen in the valley.

For birdwatchers, the bird life along the river is abundant. In the mud flat at Alum Creek you'll see various shore birds. The river is frequented by ducks, geese, and white pelicans. You may even be able to see a bald eagle, northern harrier, or Sandhill crane.

Stop by the Canyon Visitor Education Center

Located in the Canyon Village Complex, the Canyon Visitor Education Center is a part of the Mission 66 project in Yellowstone. The original visitor center was built in 1957 and the new lodge was opened the same year. You can still see remnants of the old hotel, the lodge, and other facilities.

TAKE IN THE VIEWS FROM MT. WASHBURN

Yellowstone features over 900 miles of hiking trails and one of the most popular day hikes is Mount Washburn. Located in north central Yellowstone, the mountain has a peak elevation of 10,243 feet with panoramic views up to 50 miles on a clear day. The mountain is a remnant of the volcanic activity in the region.

In addition to the views, at the top you can take in interpretive exhibits inside the base of a fire lookout. Mount Washburn is still one of three active fire lookouts in Yellowstone, and it is continuously staffed from mid-June until the end of fire season. If you come in July you'll see the slopes covered in wildflowers.

WEST THUMB AND GRANT VILLAGE

VIEW YELLOWSTONE LAKE

Yellowstone Lake was said to be shaped like a human hand, out of which the large west bay represented the thumb, leading to the area being called West Thumb. Take a day to hike and find out what are your favorite parts of the scenery.

VIEW WEST THUMB GEYSER BASIN

The West Thumb Geyser Basin, which includes Potts Basin to the north, has a unique feature– it holds the largest geyser basin on Yellowstone Lake. The heat source for this region is only 10,000 feet below the surface. The West Thumb portion of the lake is about the same size as Crater Lake in Oregon, but smaller than the huge Yellowstone caldera.

LEARN ABOUT THE EARLY INHABITANTS

Along the shore of West Thumb you'll find several Native American hearth sites that show evidence of the native people that once lived near the site and used it as a travel route, camping location, and area for food gathering.

STOP BY THE GRANT VILLAGE VISITOR CENTER

Found on the shore of West Thumb, the Grant Visitor Center is one mile off the main park road within the Grant Village Junction. The building is named after the 18th president of the United States who signed the bill to create Yellowstone National Park in 1872.

It was all finally done in the 70s, and it still is now—as it was back then— a controversial matter since the site the Center was built on is located in the middle of a grizzly bear habitat. The visitor center includes an exhibit on the role fire plays in the environment using the example of the 1988 fire. The Yellowstone Association occasionally holds sales in the lobby.

STOP BY THE WEST THUMB INFORMATION STATION

The West Thumb Ranger Station was built in 1925 and is a great example of the historic ranger station architecture in Yellowstone. In addition to an information station, the building also serves as a Yellowstone Forever sales outlet and a meeting place for interpretive walks and talks in the summer months.

In the winter, it is open as a warming hut where visitors can take shelter from the bitter cold among good company and enjoy interpretive exhibits several winter-related topics. During the spring and fall, an intermittently staffed backcountry office is located here as well.

Hike to Shoshone Lake and the Snake River

Shoshone Lake is the second largest in Yellowstone. The Snake River starts in Yellowstone and continues to the Grand Teton National Park.

Madison and West Yellowstone

Stop by the Madison Information Station

This information station dates from 1929-1930 and is now a National Historic Landmark. It is located at Madison Junction within the Madison Picnic Area and is built from both wood and stone. The buildings have been used as museums, and they also were home to the Arts Yellowstone program before being completely abandoned for a time.

It was reopened in the summer of 1995 as an information station and later on as the Yellowstone Forever bookstore.

Hike to Artists Paintpots

This is a small but beautiful thermal section just south of Norris Junction. A trail takes you through a one-mile round-trip to the hot springs, two large mud pots, and a section of forest that was burned in the 1988 fire. Nearby, you'll find three off-trail, backcountry thermal destinations: Sylvan Springs, Gibbon Hill Geyser Basin, and Geyser Creek Thermal Area.

These areas are difficult to get to, as they are fragile and dangerous, so it is advised you stay out of these sections unless you are hiking with a knowledgeable person.

Hike to Gibbon Falls

This waterfall is 84 feet and flows over the remains of the Yellowstone Caldera rim. The rock wall you see opposite the falls is the inner rim of the caldera.

Hike to Monument Geyser Basin

This nearly dormant basin is on top of a very steep one-mile trail. The geyser cones are thermos-bottle shaped and allow you to see remnants of a time when the land was more active.

Fish in the Madison River

If you like to fish schedule some time to check out the Madison River. The river forms at the junction of the Gibbon and Firehole Rivers. At Three Forks, Montana, the Madison River joins the Jefferson and the Gallatin Rivers to become the Missouri River. The Madison River is a lovely fly fishing destination with plenty of brown and rainbow trout as well as mountain whitefish.

Tour the Terrace Springs Boardwalk

Just north of Madison Junction is the small Terrace Springs thermal area. Here you can take a short boardwalk tour of the hot springs.

Fish in the Firehole River

If you're fishing in the Madison River you can save some time to head over to the Firehole River. This river starts south of Old Faithful and passes through the thermal areas to join the Gibbon River and form the Madison River. The Firehole is a popular fishing destination for brown, brook, and rainbow trout.

Drive Firehole Canyon and Swim Firehole Falls

Firehold Canyon Drive is a side road that follows the Firehole River upstream past Madison Junction to a point just above Firehole Falls. As you drive, you'll pass 800-foot thick lava flows. At the end, you can view the 40-foot Firehole Falls. This swimming spot is unstaffed and is very popular during the warmer months. Because there are no lifeguards, proceed with discretion and caution.

Mammoth Hot Springs

Stop by the Albright Visitor Center

The Albright Visitor Center is housed in the building that was originally used for quarters for single Army officers. Here you can learn about the history and wildlife in Yellowstone. You'll also be able to talk with rangers and get help planning your time in Yellowstone.

Take a Historic Tour of Fort Yellowstone

The first superintendents in the area had to deal with issues such as poaching, vandalism, and squatting. So, in 1886, the US Army arrived in Mammoth Hot Springs at the request of the Secretary of the Interior to take over control of Yellowstone. Soldiers constructed Fort Yellowstone and some of the buildings are still in use today.

Walk the Mammoth Hot Springs Terraces

You can see these steaming hydrothermals by either walking on the boardwalks or drive around the travertine terraces. In the winter, you can even ski or snowshoe among the Upper Terraces.

Take a Hike

Quite a few of the hiking trails in Yellowstone start in the Mammoth Hot Springs, including a lot of good day hikes. Plan a short day or extended hike in this area.

Always make sure you carry rain gear, extra food, and plenty of water if you plan to hike into the backcountry. Also make sure you stop by the visitor center first to find out trail conditions and bear activity.

Hike, Bike, or Drive Old Gardiner Road

This dirt road takes you to Gardiner, Montana. Cars are only allowed to travel one-way to Gardiner, but hikers and bikers can travel both ways. From this road you'll be able to observe the Yellowstone River.

Visit the Heritage and Research Center

Located in Gardiner, Montana, this state-of-the-art facility is home to Yellowstone's main museum collection, archives, research library, and the historical and archeology lab. There is a small rotating exhibit in the lobby and you can also plan ahead to take a guided behind-the-scenes tour.

Tours are often done twice a week from June to September– it is strongly recommended that you get reservations in advance.

Norris

Walk the Norris Geyser Basin Boardwalks

This is the hottest, oldest, and most dynamic thermal area in all of Yellowstone. A scientific drill hole here measured 459 degrees Fahrenheit at just 1,087 feet under the ground. Very few of the thermal features you see here are under the boiling point.

Frequent seismic activity means the features change daily in the basin. The area is also home to very rare acidic geysers. Not to mention, you'll be able to see the Steamboat Geyser, which is the tallest in the world with its explosion standing at 300 to 400 feet.

There are two specific areas to this region: Porcelain Basin and the Back Basin. There are no trees in Porcelain Basin, so it provides you with a unique sound, color, and smell experience as you walk the ¾ mile boardwalk that allows you to access the area. Back Basin is more wooded and is partially encircled by a 1.5-mile boardwalk trail.

Hike to Roaring Mountain

Just north of Norris you'll find the Norris-Mammoth section of the Grand Loop Road and off here you'll find the Roaring Mountain. This is a large acidic thermal area that features many fumaroles. It provides a unique sound experience.

Fish in the Gibbon River

The Gibbon River starts at Wolf Lake and flows through the Norris area until it meets the Firehole River at Madison Junction to become the Madison River. The majority of the flow comes from both cold and hot springs. Fly fishing is best done below Gibbon Falls and is known for its abundance of brook, brown, grayling, and rainbow trout.

Drive the Virginia Cascades

A three-mile section of the old road will take you past the 60 foot high Virginia Cascades. This waterfall is formed by the small Gibbon River. In the winter months this area is popular for cross-country skiing.

View the Norris-Canyon Blowdown

In 1984, wind shear action blew down a 22-mile section of Lodgepole pine. Then in 1988 it burned as a result of the North Fork Fire. An exhibit tells the story of how this place was heavily affected by natural disasters.

Visit the Norris Geyser Basin Museum

This building is one of the original trailside museums in the park, and it is now considered an official National Historic Landmark. It was built in 1929-1930 and has always served as a museum.

It is located ¼ mile east of Norris Junction just off the Grand Loop Road. The building itself is the distinctive stone and log architecture used throughout the rest of the park. Here you can see exhibits on geothermal geology, features of the area and life in thermal areas.

Visit the Museum of the National Park Ranger

This museum is housed in the old Norris Soldier Station at the entrance to the Norris Campground. This was originally an outlying station for soldiers patrolling the Norris Geyser Basin. It is one of the longest occupied stations in the park. An early structure was built in 1886, then replaced after a fire in 1897 and modified in 1908.

The building was used as a Ranger Station until the 1959 earthquake. Soon after, it was restored in 1991 and turned into a museum. Exhibits here show the development of the park ranger as a profession. Take a moment to watch the 25-minute movie on the story of the National Park Service development.

Old Faithful

View the Old Faithful Inn

Designed by Robert C. Reamer, who wanted the Old Faithful Inn to be asymmetrical to reflect the chaos of nature. The crooked inn was built in the winter of 1903 to 1904. This is one of the last remaining log hotels in the United States. It is a wonderful example of rustic architecture. Take the time to view the size and scope of this building while you're in the area.

Hike the Upper Geyser Basin

Nearly 60 percent of the world's geysers are found in Yellowstone. The largest number of these features are resting in the Upper Geyser Basin. Within one square mile you can count at least 150 of these. Despite this number, only five can be predicted regularly:

1. Castle
2. Grand
3. Daisy
4. Riverside
5. Old Faithful

Visit Midway Geyser Basin

While this basin is small compared to others long the Firehole River, there are unique wonders to be found. The Excelsior Geyser has a huge 200 x 300 foot crater that constantly produces over 4,000 gallons of water per minute into the river. You'll also be able to see the largest hot springs in Yellowstone, Grand Prismatic Spring. This hot spring is 370 feet in diameter and over 121 feet deep.

Visit the Lower Geyser Basin

This is another large area of hydrothermal activity that you can check out while walking along a boardwalk trail at Fountain Paint Pots or by car along the Firehole Lake Drive. The drive is a one-way, three-mile trip that passes by the Great Fountain– one of six predictable geysers. There are also several hiking trails you can take to explore this section up close.

Hike to Lone Star Geyser

The Lone Star Geyser erupts almost every three hours. Near the geyser there is a logbook in a cache for people to record observations of times and types of eruptions. The hike is an easy 4.8-mile round-trip accessible from Kepler Cascades Pullout, about 3.5 miles southeast of the Old Faithful overpass on the Grand Loop Road. If you see an eruption you should note it in the logbook and report it at the Old Faithful Visitor Education Center.

See an Old Faithful Eruption

A Yellowstone National Park tradition is to watch Old Faithful erupt. People travel from all over just to watch this geyser. In fact, it was this unique feature that inspired the establishment of this park in 1872.

Old Faithful is one of over 500 geysers in Yellowstone and only one of six that is predictable. There are special viewing areas, lodging, and concessions that you can enjoy while watching and waiting for the eruptions.

Tower-Roosevelt

Day Hike to Tower Fall

Tower Fall drops 132 feet to Tower Creek and is surrounded by eroded volcanic pinnacles. This is a popular destination for visitors and has been one of the earliest pit stops for people visiting the park.

STOP AT CALCITE SPRINGS OVERLOOK

Along the Yellowstone River you'll see the grouping of thermal springs known as Calcite Springs. This is the point marking the downstream end of the Grand Canyon of Yellowstone. This area is a popular habitat for bighorn sheep, red-tailed hawks, and osprey.

TAKE A CLASS AT THE LAMAR BUFFALO RANCH

The Lamar Buffalo Ranch features classes offered by the Yellowstone Forever Institute. The ranch was built in the early part of the century to help increase the herd size of the bison that remained in Yellowstone, preventing their extinction. Buffalo ranching continued until the 1950s. You can still find remnants of irrigation ditches, fencing, and water troughs.

There are four buildings remaining from the original ranch– two residences: the bunkhouse and the barn. All of these buildings are on the National Register of Historic Places. Old tourist cabins were brought to the area in the early 1980s to be used for Yellowstone Forever Institute Classes.

VISIT ROOSEVELT LODGE

Constructed in 1920, the Roosevelt Lodge has since been placed in the National Register of Historic Places. This also includes the Roosevelt cabins. Take a moment to visit, see the historic cabins, and sit on the porch for a few moments before continuing your journey.

ENJOY DINNER IN PLEASANT VALLEY

Pleasant Valley was once the site of Uncle John Yancey's Pleasant Valley Hotel, one of the original facilities in Yellowstone. The hotel and outbuilding were built during the period from 1884 to 1893. Today, the site is used by the park's concessioner to do "Old West" cookouts and none of the original buildings remain.

HIKE THE BANNOCK TRAIL

This trail was once used by Native Americans to access the buffalo plains in the eastern portion of the park from the Snake River plains in Idaho. After that point, the trail was used a lot from 1840 to 1876. Part of it extends from the Blacktail Plateau to where it crosses the Yellowstone River at Bannock Ford just upstream from Tower Creek.

IN-DEPTH GUIDE TO GRAND TETON NATIONAL PARK

There are four main districts to explore at Grand Teton National Park. You may be able to see all four districts in a week-long trip, but if you want to experience each activity the districts have to offer then you may want to plan multiple trips to this park. Let's look at what you can do in each of the districts.

MOOSE DISTRICT

The Moose District is found in the southern part of Grand Teton National Park about 12 miles north of Jackson, Wyoming. In this district you can enjoy a range of trails, activities, scenic drives, and ranger programs. There are also several unique historic districts and iconic views of the Teton Range. Start your visit at the Craig Thomas Discovery and Visitor Center to get help planning your trip, get the necessary permits, and view informative exhibits.

Stop by Menor's Ferry Historic District and Mormon Row in order to travel back in time. For viewing the wilderness head to Murie Ranch. For mountain hikes, trek to Taggart, Bradley, and Phelps Lakes. Head into Death Canyon if you want to explore the alpine backcountry. Take a scenic drive to look for bison, moose, and pronghorn.

A multi-use pathway exists for bicycles that runs north from Jackson and parallels the main highway, then turns west at Trailheads and travels for eight miles to South Jenny Lake at the base of the Teton Range. There are also plenty of water activities offered along Snake River including floating, fishing, and swimming.

If you choose to camp in this district, there is the Gros Ventre Campground along the Gros Ventre River. This campground doesn't accept reservations, so you will need to arrive early to get a site.

The area is surrounded by cottonwood and spruce trees with moose and bison as regular visitors. There are 300 sites, 36 with electric hookups, and 5 group sites.

COLTER BAY

This bay is in the northern portion of the Grand Teton National Park about 25 miles north of Moose District and 20 miles south of Yellowstone National Park. There are a variety of trails, scenic drives, and ranger programs to enjoy along with gorgeous vistas of the Teton Range on the other side of Jackson Lake.

Start your trip at the Colter Bay Visitor Center to acquire maps and an ideal route for your adventure, you can also view current exhibits. You'll find geology and climate panels as well as new orientation displays. 17 miles north of Colter Bay you'll find the Flagg Ranch Information Station which provides a quick overview of the park. While this district is open year-round to vehicles, the visitor center is only open from early May to early October.

There are numerous hiking trails that you can explore. Hike along the shores of the Jackson Lake, Two Ocean, or Emma Matilda Lakes, or head north along the Snake River at Flagg Ranch. There are four trailheads in this district:

1. Hermitage Point
2. Flagg Ranch
3. Jackson Lake Lodge
4. Two Ocean

If you would like to get out on the lake, head to the Colter Bay Marina where you can launch your own boat or you can rent a canoe, kayak, or even a motorboat to head out on the lake. Non-motorized boats can access Snake River or Two Ocean Lake. Boat permits are required and can be obtained at the Colter Bay Permits Office.

Another popular water activity is floating down the Snake River. Several private companies offer float trips down the river. There are several launch sites that offer varying levels of difficulty.

You can also fish along Snake River for cutthroat trout or head out onto Jackson Lake. Make sure you purchase a Wyoming fishing license.

Colter Bay offers an RV Park with 112 sites that accept reservations through the Grand Teton Lodge Company. The Colter Bay Campground doesn't take reservations and sits above Jackson Lake within a Lodgepole forest. There are 335 individual sites, 13 with electric hookups and 11 group sites.

There is also the Lizard Creek Campground nine miles north of Colter Bay that looks over Jackson Lake. It is a small campground with only 60 sites. A second RV park is available 16 miles north of Colter Bay at Flagg Ranch at Headwaters.

Common wildlife in this area for includes moose, bears, wolves, elk, mule deer, Sandhill cranes, pelicans, and osprey.

Drive through this northern portion of the park to see the view and potentially catch a glimpse of the surrounding wildlife. The highway north of Moran Junction passes Oxbow Bend before it reaches Jackson Lake Junction.

Turn to the west if you want to approach Jackson Lake Dam or you can head north to Jackson Lake Lodge. As you continue north past Colter Bay you can come face to face to the panorama of the northern Teton Range and Jackson Lake before you drive up Huckleberry Hill and then drop down into Flagg Ranch.

JENNY LAKE

This district gives you easy access to valley lakes and several moderate to strenuous hikes while taking in beautiful mountain scenery. Some of the most popular hikes in the park are found in this district, which is open for vehicle traffic from May 1st to October 31st.

Hiking in the Jenny Lake District allows you to hike to lakes and canyons, follow creeks, and get up close to the central Tetons. There are four trailheads within five miles. Visit the Ranger station first for current route conditions and to get any needed backcountry permits during peak summer months.

There is also a biking path that starts from South Jenny Lake and takes you eight miles south along the base of the Teton Range to Dornan's in the Moose District.

At Jenny Lake you can launch your own boat or rent a canoe or kayak from Jenny Lake Boating. You will need to get a boating permit, however. Sailboats and wind surfers aren't allowed here, but can go to Jackson Lake. For a more private experience, head to String Lake which connects to Leigh Lake.

Fishing for cutthroat and lake trout is allowed on Jenny Lake, but is prohibited at the downstream Cottonwood Creek. Downstream of the creek is Exum Bridge which is open to fishing from August 1st to October 31st. You'll need to buy a Wyoming fishing license.

The Jenny Lake District also offers the experience of climbing. People come from around the world to climb the Teton Range. You'll need to get a permit from the

Ranger Station and find current route conditions before heading out to the mountains.

The Jenny Lake Campground doesn't accept reservations and often fills by 9am so you should get there early. It is limited to 50 tent sites and offers you short walk access to the lake. If this campground is full, you can head north on the Teton Park Road for nine miles to reach the Signal Mountain Campground. There are 81 tent sites and room for RVs up to 30 feet in length at this location. This campground often fills by noon.

There are many animals that frequent the district. Common mammals seen around here include moose, bears, elk, mule deer, pika, marmot, and ground squirrels. Common birds include eagles, osprey, and woodpeckers.

There are two memorable scenic drives in this district that you should consider completion if you have time. There is the Jenny Lake scenic loop and the Signal Mountain Summit road. Stop at the Cathedral Group Turnout and the Jenny Lake Overlook if you want to enjoy some marvelous landscapes.

LAURANCE S. ROCKEFELLER DISTRICT

This district or preserve is located four miles south of the Moose District along the Moose-Wilson Road. It is a special place where you can connect with nature in an area specifically-designed to reduce congestion. The road to this portion of the park is closed to RVs and trailers over 23 feet in length and is unpaved for 1.5 miles.

Parking is limited and often fills before 9am and remains full until after 4pm. The district is accessible by vehicle from May 1st to October 31st with the Center open from late May through September.

The destination offers an eight-mile trail network that provides you with views of Phelps Lake, Death Canyon, and the Teton Range. You'll be able to hike through mature forests and aspen groves.

You can fish from the shores of Phelps Lake with a Wyoming fishing license. A wash station is provided in the parking lot to avoid the spread of aquatic nuisance species.

There are no campgrounds in this area of the park, but there are three backcountry campsites on the north end of the lake. If you are staying here, you can't park your cars overnight in the parking lot.

This is a prime place to view wildlife such as: moose, bears, mule deer, eagles, and owls.

IN-DEPTH GUIDE TO GLACIER NATIONAL PARK

Glacier National Park is a wonderful place to visit. With a lot of outdoor activities and a lot of hiking trails you can easily spend a whole week exploring just one section of the park.

Let's take an in-depth look at all sections of the park and you can plan a trip to see the main sights you are the most interested in, then you can book a return trip to catch everything you missed.

LAKE MCDONALD VALLEY

This location is the hub for activity on the west side of Glacier National Park. At one time, this area was occupied by massive glaciers thousands of years ago. Now this valley is filled with beautiful views, hiking trails, and a wide range of animal and plant species. You should also enjoy the historic chalets and the grand Lake McDonald Lodge.

Lake McDonald is the largest lake in the park at nearly 10 miles long and almost 500 feet deep. This lake is the direct result of glacial carving. The glaciers also carved the u-shaped valley the lake sits in along with the smaller hanging valleys with waterfalls that you can access by the many hiking trails.

Along the shore of the lake you'll find Lake McDonald Lodge. Built in 1913 to 1914, it resembles a rustic hunting lodge with a Swiss style architecture. Spend your days hiking, horseback riding, or taking a scenic boat tour on the DeSmet, a historic boat.

FACILITIES, SERVICES, AND ACTIVITIES

- ☐ Apgar Visitor Center
- ☐ Camping:

    - ☐ Apgar
    - ☐ Avalanche
    - ☐ Fish Creek
    - ☐ Sprague Creek

- ☐ Ranger Guided Programs
- ☐ Day Hikes
- ☐ Guided Hiking and Backpacking Tours
- ☐ Lodging
- ☐ Restaurants
- ☐ General Stores and Gift Shops
- ☐ Boat Rentals
- ☐ Road Tours
- ☐ Horseback Tours
- ☐ Picnic Areas
- ☐ Drinking Water
- ☐ Restrooms
- ☐ Shuttle Service

HIKES

- ☐ Apgar Bike Path, 1.5 miles one-way– Mostly level asphalt path south of the Apgar Backcountry Permit Office.
- ☐ Apgar Lookout, 3.6 miles one-way – Turn left a half-mile north of the West Entrance and continue 1.5 miles beyond Quarter Circle Bridge to reach the trailhead.

- ☐ Avalanche Lake, 2.3 miles one-way – Trailhead at Avalanche Picnic Area.
- ☐ Fish Creek Bike Path, 1.2 miles one way – Turn right 0.25 miles north of the Lower McDonald Creek Bridge along Camas Road for the trailhead.
- ☐ Fish Lake, 2.7 miles one-way – Starts at Sperry Trailhead.
- ☐ Forest and Fire Nature Trail, 1.1-mile loop – Trailhead located off the Camas Road parking area near the Camas Creek Entrance.
- ☐ Howe Lake, 1.6 miles one-way – Start at Howe Lake Trailhead off Inside North Fork Road.
- ☐ Huckleberry Lookout, 6 miles one-way – Starts at Huckleberry Mountain Trailhead off Camas Road.
- ☐ Johns Lake Loop, 3 miles one-way – Starts at Johns Lake Trailhead.
- ☐ Lake McDonald West Shore, 7.4 miles one-way – Two trailheads either 0.2 miles north of the Fish Creek Campground or 2.8 miles west of North Lake McDonald Road.
- ☐ Lincoln Lake, 8 miles one-way – Starts from Lincoln Lake parking area off Going-to-the-Sun Road.
- ☐ Mount Brown Lookout, 5.2 miles one-way – Starts from Sperry Trailhead.
- ☐ Oxbow Trail, 1.5 miles one-way – Starts at the south side of Lower McDonald Creek Bridge off Camas Road.
- ☐ Rocky Point, 1.1 miles one-way – Starts 0.2 miles north of Fish Creek Campground.
- ☐ Snyder Lakes, 4.3 miles one-way – Starts at Sperry Trailhead.
- ☐ Sperry Chalet, 6.3 miles one-way – Starts at Sperry Trailhead.
- ☐ Trail of the Cedars, 0.7 miles one-way – Wheelchair accessible. Starts from the Avalanche Picnic Area.
- ☐ Trout Lake, 4 miles one-way – Starts from Trout Lake Trailhead.

LOGAN PASS

At this area of the park you will find Reynolds Mountain and Clements Mountain towering over you as you walk through fields of wildflowers in the summer.

Wildlife viewing opportunities here includes mountain goats, bighorn sheep, and occasionally grizzly bears.

Drive up to Logan Pass and you'll reach the highest elevation point in the park by vehicle at 6,646 feet. This pass is popular with visitors and the lot often fills between 8:30am and 4pm. There are free shuttles that take you here so you can avoid the limited parking. The two most popular trails are the Hidden Lake Trail and the Highline Trail.

Facilities, Services, and Activities

- ☐ Logan Pass Visitor Center
- ☐ Ranger Guided Programs
- ☐ Day Hikes
- ☐ Guided Hiking and Backpacking Tours
- ☐ Drinking Water
- ☐ Restrooms
- ☐ Shuttle Service

Hikes

- ☐ Granite Park Chalet, 7.6 miles – Accessed by Highline Trail or by the Swiftcurrent Trailhead.
- ☐ Hidden Lake Overlook, 1.4 miles – Starts at Logan Pass Visitor Center.

Many Glacier

There are a few things you need to know before visiting this area of the park. First, the access road into this valley is rough and has a lot of potholes, so you need to use caution when driving a vehicle with low clearance. Second, parking is limited at the ranger station. Lastly, on some busy days access to the valley is restricted until parking is available.

This is often considered the heart of Glacier National Park. The mountains are huge, the glaciers are active, the lakes are crystal clear, there are numerous hiking trails, and a wide variety of wildlife. It is also one of the destinations in the park where you can choose to travel by vehicle, foot, boat, or horseback to get an up-close view of glaciers and how they impact the landscape.

This is also the section of the park to visit if you want to fill your days with hikes. Trails spread out in all directions. The two most popular hikes you should make time for are the Grinnell Glacier Trail and the Iceberg Lake Trail.

Even with a week to spare you won't be able to cover all the hiking trails in this area, which is why planning beforehand might allow you to see the main ones.

During the spring, the bighorn sheep graze close to the road, and late summer is peak season for both grizzly and black bears so take appropriate caution and do not leave any food behind or the bears will follow you.

FACILITIES, SERVICES, AND ACTIVITIES

- ☐ Camping
    - ☐ Many Glacier Campground
- ☐ Ranger Guided Programs
- ☐ Day Hikes
- ☐ Guided Hiking and Backpacking Tours
- ☐ Lodging
- ☐ Restaurants

- ☐ General Store & Gift Shops
- ☐ Scenic Boat Tours and Rentals
- ☐ Road Tours
- ☐ Horseback Tours
- ☐ Showers
- ☐ Picnic Areas
- ☐ Drinking Water
- ☐ Restrooms

HIKES

- ☐ Apikuni Falls, one mile one-way – Starts from Apikuni Parking Area.
- ☐ Cracker Lake, 6.4 miles one-way – Starts from south end of Many Glacier Hotel Parking Lot.
- ☐ Grinnell Glacier Viewpoint, 5.3 miles one-way – Starts from Grinnell Glacier Trailhead or the Many Glacier Hotel.
- ☐ Grinnell Glacier Viewpoint, 3.6 miles one-way – By boat from the Many Glacier Hotel.
- ☐ Grinnell Lake, 3.4 miles one-way – Starts at Grinnell Glacier Trailhead or the Many Glacier Hotel.
- ☐ Grinnell Lake, 1.1 mile one-way – By boat from the Many Glacier Hotel.
- ☐ Iceberg Lake, 4.8 miles one-way – Starts from Iceberg Ptarmigan Trailhead.
- ☐ Piegan Pass, 4.5 miles one-way – Starts from Piegan Pass Trailhead.
- ☐ Piegan Pass, 8.4 miles one-way – Starts from the south end of the Many Glacier Hotel Parking Lot.
- ☐ Poia Lake, 6.4 miles one-way – Starts from Apikuni Parking Area.
- ☐ Ptarmigan Falls, 2.7 miles one-way – Starts at Iceberg Ptarmigan Trailhead.
- ☐ Ptarmigan Lake, 4.3 miles one-way – Starts at Iceberg Ptarmigan Trailhead.

- ☐ Ptarmigan Tunnel, 5.3 miles one-way – Starts at Iceberg Ptarmigan Trailhead.
- ☐ Redrock Falls, 1.8 miles one-way – Starts at Swiftcurrent Trailhead.
- ☐ Swiftcurrent Nature Trail, 2.3-mile loop – Starts at Grinnell Glacier Trailhead or the Many Glacier Hotel.
- ☐ Swiftcurrent Pass, 6.8 miles one-way – Starts at Swiftcurrent Trailhead.

ST. MARY VALLEY

The valley is the eastern gateway to Glacier National Park. Here you'll find a landscape that includes a vast array of prairies, mountains, and forests. This makes for a habitat with diverse plants and animals. St. Mary Lake spans about 10 miles.

Driving along the lake provides you with many beautiful sights. You can also enjoy learning about Native American history since this part of the park borders Blackfeet Reservation.

FACILITIES, SERVICES, AND ACTIVITIES

- ☐ St. Mary Visitor Center
- ☐ Camping

    - ☐ Rising Sun
    - ☐ St. Mary

- ☐ Ranger Guided Programs
- ☐ Day Hikes
- ☐ Guided Hiking and Backpacking Tours
- ☐ Lodging
- ☐ Restaurant

- ☐ General Store & Gift Shop
- ☐ Scenic Boat Tours
- ☐ Road Tours
- ☐ Showers
- ☐ Picnic Areas
- ☐ Drinking Water
- ☐ Restrooms
- ☐ Pit Toilets
- ☐ Shuttle Service

HIKES

- ☐ Baring Falls, 0.3 miles one-way – Starts at Sunrift Gorge Pullout.
- ☐ Beaver Pond Loop, 3.3 miles – Starts at 1913 Ranger Station.
- ☐ Otokomi Lake, 5.5 miles one-way – Starts at the Rising Sun Camp Store.
- ☐ Piegan Pass, 4.5 miles one-way – Starts at Piegan Pass Trailhead.
- ☐ Piegan Pass, 8.4 miles one-way – Starts at the south end of the Many Glacier Hotel Parking Lot.
- ☐ Red Eagle Lake, 8.1 miles one-way – Starts at 1913 Ranger Station Parking Area.
- ☐ St. Mary Falls, 0.8 miles one-way – Starts at St. Mary Falls Shuttle Stop.
- ☐ St. Mary Falls, 1.2 miles one-way – Starts at St. Mary Falls Trailhead.
- ☐ St. Mary Falls, 1.6 miles one-way – By boat from Rising Sun.
- ☐ Siyeh Pass, 4.6 miles one-way – Starts at Piegan Pass Trailhead.
- ☐ Siyeh Pass, 5.5 miles one-way – Starts at Sunrift Gorge Pullout.
- ☐ Sun Point Nature Trail, 0.8 miles one-way – Starts at Sunrift Gorge Pullout.
- ☐ Sunrift Gorge, 200 feet one-way – Starts at Sunrift Gorge Pullout.
- ☐ Virginia Falls, 1.6 miles one-way – Starts at St. Mary Falls Shuttle Stop.
- ☐ Virginia Falls, 1.8 miles one-way – Starts at St. Mary Falls Trailhead.
- ☐ Virginia Falls, 2.4 miles one-way – By boat from Rising Sun.

Two Medicine

This was once the primary destination for those arriving to the park by train. After spending a night at the Glacier Park Lodge, people then traveled by horse to Two Medicine for a night in a rustic chalet or canvas tipis. From Two Medicine, a system of backcountry tent camps and chalets allows people to explore the interior of the park.

Both backpackers and day hikers will find beautiful scenery in this area and provides people with a true wilderness experience. You can also take a casual boat tour of Two Medicine Lake.

Facilities, Services and Activities

- ☐ Camping
    - ☐ Two Medicine Campground

- ☐ Ranger Guided Programs
- ☐ Day Hikes
- ☐ Guided Hiking and Backpacking Tours
- ☐ General Store & Gift Shop
- ☐ Scenic Boat Tours
- ☐ Road Tours
- ☐ Picnic Areas
- ☐ Drinking Water
- ☐ Restrooms

Hikes

- ☐ Appistoki Falls, 0.6 miles one-way – Starts at Scenic Point Parking Area.
- ☐ Aster Falls, 1.2 mile one-way – Starts at South Shore Trailhead.

- ☐ Aster Park, 2 miles one-way – Starts at South Shore Trailhead.
- ☐ Cobalt Lake, 5.8 miles one-way – Starts at South Shore Trailhead.
- ☐ Dawson Pass, 6.5 miles one-way – Starts at North Shore Trailhead.
- ☐ No Name Lake, 4.9 miles one-way – Starts at North Shore Trailhead.
- ☐ Oldman Lake, 6.4 miles one-way – Starts at North Shore Trailhead.
- ☐ Paradise Point, 0.7 miles one-way – Starts at South Shore Trailhead.
- ☐ Pitamakan Pass, 7.6 miles one-way – Starts at North Shore Trailhead.
- ☐ Rockwell Falls, 3.5 miles one-way – Starts at South Shore Trailhead.
- ☐ Running Eagle Falls, 0.3 miles one-way – Starts at Running Eagle Falls Trailhead. Wheelchair accessible.
- ☐ Scenic Point, 3.9 miles one-way – Starts at Scenic Point Parking Area.
- ☐ Twin Falls, 3.5 miles one-way – Starts at North Shore Trailhead.
- ☐ Twin Falls, 0.9 miles one-way – By boat from South Shore Trailhead.
- ☐ Upper Two Medicine Lake, 5 miles one-way – Starts at North Shore Trailhead.
- ☐ Upper Two Medicine Lake, 2.2 miles one-way – By boat from South Shore Trailhead.

CUT BANK

Located off Highway 89 between Two Medicine and St. Mary.

HIKES

- ☐ Medicine Grizzly Lake, 6 miles one-way – Starts at Cut Bank Trailhead.
- ☐ Morning Star Lake, 6.6 miles one-way – Starts at Cut Bank Trailhead.
- ☐ Triple Divide Pass, 7.2 miles one-way – Starts at Cut Bank Trailhead.

WALTON

This district is off Highway 2 near the south boundary of the park.

Hikes

- ☐ Firebrand Pass, 4.8 miles one-way – Starts at Lubec Trailhead.
- ☐ Scalplock Lookout, 4.7 miles one-way – Starts at Walton Ranger Station.

North Fork

This is a section of the park that sees reduced crowds and is located in the northwest corner of Glacier National Park. You can only get to this part through the use of a private vehicle on unpaved roads. Here you'll be able to observe Bowman and Kintla Lakes as well as the remains of old homesteading sites.

However, because of its remote location, it also has limited services and requires visitors to be self-reliant. It is also recommended to have a spare tire as flat tires are a common problem.

Facilities, Services, and Activities

- ☐ Camping
    - ☐ Bowman Lake
    - ☐ Logging Creek
    - ☐ Kintla Lake
    - ☐ Quartz Creek

- ☐ Day Hikes
- ☐ Picnic Areas
- ☐ Drinking Water
- ☐ Restrooms
- ☐ Pit Toilets

HIKES

- ☐ Akokala Lake, 5.8 miles one-way – Starts at Bowman Lake Ranger Station.
- ☐ Bowman Lake Head, 7.1 miles one-way – Starts at Bowman Lake Ranger Station.
- ☐ Covey Meadow, 1.5 mile one-way – Starts at Polebridge Ranger Station.
- ☐ Hidden Meadow, 1.2 mile one-way – Starts 3 miles south of Polebridge Ranger Station.
- ☐ Kintla Lake Head, 6.6 miles one-way – Starts 0.25 mile west of Kintla Lake Campground.
- ☐ Logging Lake, 4.5 miles one-way – Starts north of Logging Creek Ranger Station.
- ☐ Lower Quartz Lake, 3 miles one-way – Starts at Bowman Lake Picnic Area.
- ☐ Lower Quartz Lake, 6.9 miles one-way – Starts north of Quartz Creek Campground.
- ☐ Numa Lookout, 5.6 miles one-way – Starts at Bowman Lake Ranger Station.
- ☐ Quartz Lake, 6 miles one-way – Starts at Bowman Lake Picnic Area.

GOAT HAUNT

This is another remote and peaceful area of the park which allows you to explore Glacier without the crowds. Many visitors choose to take a boat from Waterton Lakes National Park in Canada, but you can also walk into this destination. You'll notice the straight swath of cut trees that mark the International Boundary.

The unique ecosystem in this area is a great place to record rare, unique wildlife and plant species. There are no services in this area of the park, so the nearby towns are the place for that task.

Facilities, Services, and Activities

- ☐ Day Hikes
- ☐ Guided Hiking and Backpacking Tours
- ☐ Scenic Boat Tours
- ☐ Drinking Water
- ☐ Restrooms
- ☐ Ranger Station

Hikes

- ☐ Goat Haunt Overlook, 1 mile one-way – Starts at Ranger Station.
- ☐ Kootenai Lakes, 2.5 miles one-way – Starts at Ranger Station.
- ☐ Lake Francis, 6.2 miles one-way – Starts at Ranger Station.
- ☐ Lake Janet, 3.3 miles one-way – Starts at Ranger Station.
- ☐ Rainbow Falls, 1 mile one-way – Starts at Ranger Station.
- ☐ Waterton Townsite, 8.5 miles one-way – Starts at Ranger Station.

LAST WORD

These are only a few of the many national parks scattered all throughout the United States, but they are incredibly worthwhile. They are natural landmarks for a reason, after all; it is not every day that one can find the largest living tree on Earth or a waterfall that looks as though it is flowing with liquid flaming gold. There is so much to see in this world, and these locations remind us of our insignificance compared to the powerful ground below us.

The earthy scent of falling rain, the crackle of gravel beneath our feet, the sensation of sunlight coating your skin. You cannot find that within the screen of a laptop or a phone.

Every now and then, it is a fundamental part of life to press a pause button on the world with day-to-day commodities and technology, and simply become one with nature, as we were once so many years ago. Being able to look top of a mountain at the world below you after hours of sweat and a burning feeling in your muscles during that last strenuous mile is one of the best, most unforgettable moments you will ever experience.

If hiking is not that much of a hobby or a way of life for you, simply taking a walk or photographing what you see in order to capture a single second of the sheer world of wonders in front of you is also more than enough.

Hopefully, this guide allowed you to brainstorm plans and future long-term trips to either of these national parks with friends, family, or even by your own accord as you search once again for the ultimate human connection to the planet we live in. Thank you, and best of luck in your adventures.

If you are interested in reading and learning about the all the National Parks in the Eastern United States, looks for my third and final book in this series.

Lastly, I want to say THANK YOU for purchasing and reading my book. I really hope you got a lot out of it!

Can I ask you for a quick favor though?

If you enjoyed this book, I would really appreciate it if you could leave me a Review.

I LOVE getting feedback from my wonderful readers, and reviews really do make the difference. I read all of my reviews and would love to hear your thoughts.

I also want to ask for your help and forgiveness ahead of time, in the event if you find any errors, typos or outdated information, please feel free to email me so I can fix the mistake.

bushcrafttrainer@gmail.com

Last but not the least, I want to extend my heartfelt thanks to http://commons.wikimedia.org and flickr.com

Thank you so much!!

Rob J. Simms

Made in the USA
Las Vegas, NV
25 March 2022